CW01649703

The Angel Guardian Copy

Book Of Sorothir 2

Joshua Mortimer

The Angel Guardian (Book Of Sorothir 2)
by Joshua Mortimer

Cover by Ambient Designs
Logo by Peter Evans
Edited by Emily Wright
Published by Joshua Mortimer
ISBN: 978-1-9989980-3-6 (Book)
1st Edition

To Esther, Aoife, Jasper and Niamh

Chapter One

"The magic within this book is more commonly known as Blood Magic, which was thought to have been lost, but it is more accurate to call it Demon Magic."
The Book of Sorothir

A Long Time Ago...

Having visited her friend Silevaith of Angelic Order Arndell, Sorothir had decided to explore a tall grey mountain range close by Castle Arndell. Flying up along the sharp crags, which peppered the steep incline, she landed on a bare plateau near the top.

At the back of the plateau was a small cave.

Staring at it and contemplating her next movements, Sorothir's cloak whipped about her in the strong winds of the rocky mountain.

Oh, how different her Order lived, compared to Angelic Order Arndell, she chided herself. She was used to residing in a city filled with skyscrapers that twinkled at night, to give the feeling of something magical. In this barren and harsh wilderness, there was no wonder her friend Silevaith had turned out to be so stoic. A smile spread across her face at that thought.

When Sorothir was younger, she had never appreciated why Arch Uraih had kept Angelic Order Nisassah, in such a place to live, amongst the mortals. But she soon learned it was because of the easy supply of equipment and chemicals, which her Order thrived on for their experiments. The mortals may be weak and soft, but they were adept at creating resources for the shadow world to use.

Sorothir, standing on the wind-swept plateau wrapped her cloak about her tighter, and strode towards the cave. Exploring untrodden pastures, was ingrained in her Order's blood, to seek and find new things, it had been the only way her Nisassah had survived against the larger Angelic Orders. Perhaps she would find something useful in this cave for her Order.

Stopping at the entrance and peering in, she could make out little of the inside for it was pitch black. Clicking her torch on and shining it into the darkness, she was relieved to find no wolves or other dangerous animals in there. She would have hated to fight a harmless creature, that was only defending its home. Crossing into the cave's embrace, her feet crunched on loose gravel. Once she was in a few metres, her torch located how the cave curved out of sight to the left.

The further she went in, the flooring turned to large rocks until her torch shone onto a dead end of smooth rock.

That was a shame. She sighed and ran her hand across it.

"That feels different." Sorothir rubbed her finger and thumb together. There had been some sort of current, as though static coursed through her.

She shone the torch closer to the smooth rock and squinted at it. There was nothing obvious on the surface, just the veins of differing grey rock going horizontal.

She placed her hand on the rock and again, felt the static feeling coursing through.

If there was some current running through it, maybe she could send it back to its source. She unscrewed the back of her torch, exposing the two batteries inside and pitching her into darkness. Then taking a knife which was concealed in her boot, she placed the edge against the fake wall.

"Here goes nothing," she murmured. Then placing the exposed batteries of the torch against the side of the knife to complete the circuit, a strange noise sounded within the cave.

Heart pounding, she replaced her knife back in her boot, then rummaged around in a pocket for the end of the torch, finally pulling it free from the lose fabric within and screwed it back on.

The light came on straight away, making her recoil from the brightness. She blinked trying to adjust her eyes. When her sight sufficiently returned, she could see that the back wall was now gone. It had disappeared completely with no trace of rocks anywhere. It was as though it had been created by magic, to stop anyone from passing. For what purpose though?

Even though Sorothir's legs felt like jelly, she whispered to herself. "Be brave."

Sorothir took a step forward with her numb legs, moving one foot at a time and for good measure, she withdrew her dagger, clenching it in a vice-like grip. Waving her torch back and forwards to make sure nothing hid in the shadows, it eventually fell into the blackness of a high cavern.

Her mouth fell agape. The cavern was tall, and sharp spikes threatened to impale her from above and below. The occasional drip fell into small puddles on the floor, causing a light thud.

At the back of the small cavern was a crevice, that went from floor to ceiling. So, Sorothir made her way towards it, jumping over large puddles to avoid her black boots from getting drenched. One such puddle she jumped over, she mistimed, and the heel of her foot slid into the water hitting something loose within. Crouching down and peering in, the torch fell onto something.

Sorothir scraped a knife against the bottom, trying to pull the object up. On the third attempt, a long white rock spilled out of the water onto the side. Turning it over with the knife, there was a large round smooth area on the back. That wasn't a rock! She stood up and swung her torch around the room, making sure she was alone. That was bone!

Had the fake cave wall from earlier, imbued with some form of magic, been created to stop someone from finding it? Or to keep something inside?

Sorothir took a deep breath. "I've come too far to turn back now, get a grip of yourself. Just a few more moments."

She promised herself, she would just see what lay beyond the large crack at the back of the cavern, then she would turn back home.

Standing on the threshold of the large crevice, the rock inside was visibly red and orange. Different from the grey rock of the rest of the cave.

Sorothir took a deep breath and stepped through, and as she did so, she felt the searing heat hit her.

"What is this?"Sorothir said to herself. Looking behind her, she saw the cavern was still behind her, but it was now shimmering, as though an invisible curtain was in the way.

"It can't be, can it? A portal." Holding her hand up, to feel the breeze of heat which warmed her.

The passageway on this side, was flanked by orange and red jagged rocks, threatening to bite into her. She made her way through, taking care that her steps landed on solid footing.

The going was tough and at times frightening. Before the path widened Sorothir had to squeeze past a boulder which blocked her path.

Peering around the edge of the obstruction her heart leapt into her mouth.

Her biggest fear while exploring this side of the portal, was to encounter something living. And now her fears had come true.

Three things as tall as her, were clustered together further along the path, eating something that lay on the floor.

They almost seemed human, if it weren't for their twisted bodies. All three were different colours but mostly dominated by yellow, orange, reds and green.

Sorothir's hand went to her mouth. "Oh no." She whispered to herself, "demons!"

Even though angels still whispered about demons, they hadn't been seen for a long time and no one really knew how to get to the demon realm. Or if they did, then it was a closely guarded secret.

But there in front of Sorothir, there was no denying it, there were demons.

She listened as the hideous creatures tore into flesh, and gave an involuntary shudder. It was time to go now, Sorothir said to herself.

She turned to leave but in doing so, her foot slipped on a pebble, scraping her boot buckle along the floor.

The noise of eating stopped and in the red light that permeated into the passageway, three heads were staring at her.

Oh no! She drew a short sword, sharp and handy in close environments. And clearing all thoughts of doubt that crept in, she took one breath and headed towards them at a sprint. Underneath her feet, small pebbles shifted, so she adjusted her weight, trying to tread lightly. At two paces away from her target, the closest demon lifted its twisted face. Before it could open its mouth to screech a warning, with those sharp needle-like teeth that lined its mouth, she planted the sword into its neck. With a twist of her wrist, the blade widened the hole and tore free.

With just enough time to side step past an outstretched hand of a second demon, Sorothir made her way deeper into the cave. She slashed at its claws, making it screech. One down, two to go.

She didn't dare look back as she sprinted. Ahead, in the limited light that penetrated the cave, she made out a small archway. It was tall enough for her to get through and only just wide enough for two people to walk through. She ran towards it and almost came to a stop when she realised that the light in the cavern was coming from glowing stones embedded in the rockface. Their dull glow shining light on the two demons approaching, one holding its hand close to its chest.

The demons were slightly different, one was orange, with spikes jutting along its jaw line, its muscles and tendons on show. While the one holding its injured hand, was thinner and sinewy. They approached without checking their speed, intent on only one thing. Armed with just her short sword, Sorothir knew she was vulnerable to a frontal charge. The demons would be stronger than her, and if they ran side by side, she may finish one off, but the other would surely topple and kill her. Thankfully though, the demons did not work as a pack, they came, one in front of the other.

When the lead demon was a few steps away. Sorothir side-stepped and ducked at the same time, to avoid their outstretched claws. The demon darted past and as it tried to slow and turn, Sorothir jumped at its back, stabbing it in the side of the head. She realised as she did it though, it was a mistake. She had stabbed with such force, that her short sword was now embedded in the lifeless head of the demon, and there was no time to wrench it free. Sorothir leapt over the dead demon and turned just in time to see the third and last of the demons, the one clutching its wounded hand to its chest, make a grab for her. But with the dead demon in between, she was just out of reach and she knew she had seconds before it leapt at her. It sneered, licking its lips with a long thin black tongue. Searching frantically around, she tried to find something that might help. There was nothing there except...

Before the demon could move, she crouched down, grabbed a handful of dirt from the tunnel floor and flung it into the demon's eyes. The demon clawed at its face and screeched out in frustration.

Sorothir launched herself at the short sword embedded in the demon on the floor and with two hands, and bracing her foot, she yanked, and to her relief the sword broke free.

Jumping to her feet, Sorothir kicked at the demons' legs, causing it to fall.

Then with one last groan, Sorothir hefted the short sword high in the air and stabbed it downwards. A bloody ooze spilled onto the floor from the dying demon.

Sorothir bent over double, sucking in deep breaths.

"What are you doing Sorothir." She berated herself and smacked her sword in frustration against the dirt of the cave. She shouldn't have come this far without a plan. She would go home, back through the portal. And next time, she would come back better prepared, to find the secrets of this place. The demon realm.

Chapter Two

Present Day...

Rafe paced his room, not able to keep still, after returning from visiting Evie in hospital where she still lay motionless after four weeks. His fingers fidgeted anxiously and his mind buzzed with a thousand thoughts.

He'd occasionally spied Evie's parents at the hospital, who'd seemed to have patched up their differences to care for their only daughter, unconscious and hooked up to life support machines. Rafe wished he could have eased their burden and told them how a cursed knife had been thrown at her in HOG, but The Fates forbade it. He dared not cross them and even if he wanted to, he was almost sure they'd cast some sort of glamour to avoid awkward questions being asked.

Rafe had no idea what he was meant to do. Or could do.

His mission with The Fates had lasted most of summer, and school had started a few weeks back. His teachers had spoken to his parents, noticing

Rafe had withdrawn into himself. They'd asked if everything was okay at home and his parents had tried to sit with him to discuss it. At first, they'd been sympathetic, then they got frustrated. Now they simply ignored it, hoping it would go away. They hadn't known Evie, how could they, he'd only become friends with her recently and that was in the timeline.

Sometimes he thought all he wanted was to be hugged and told it would be okay. While other times, just to be left alone but in all honesty, he didn't know what he wanted. His best friend, Rory, had asked him once, but Rafe didn't want to speak to him about it either. From then on, Rory knew better than to ask again, and like his parents, he too ignored it.

That morning he had gone to hospital to talk to Evie. He didn't know if she could hear, although he always felt better after telling her everything that was on his mind. He'd been to visit the last two weekends, sat by her side alone, then when visiting hours were over, he would vanish before anyone could speak to him. On those occasions, he had gone in his normal clothes, while today was a special day, it was her birthday. He didn't know why he had given her a birthday card, it wasn't as if she could enjoy it. Maybe she would wake up one day soon, and see the card from him.

As he had sat there, he talked inwardly at how Evie was brave as hell, she had chosen to stay with Rafe to help The Fates for the greater good. And now she paid the ultimate sacrifice, stuck half way between life and death. He'd wondered a little guiltily if perhaps he was the intended target.

He'd grown close to her over the limited time they'd spent together. He'd started to peel back the barriers she put up, learning that things at home weren't so rosy and she needed a friend. And he was glad, proud even, that he had become that friend for her. There was also a touch of regret, at not having reached out sooner to her, and for not giving her the chance until it was too late. From then on, he vowed to himself that no matter what, he would always give time to anyone that needed it. He couldn't live with anymore guilt or regret, as everyone deserved a chance and a friend.

Sometime during his pacing, he must have found his way to the edge of the bed for now he began to lean back, feeling a little tired. He was about to sit down, when he heard something.

"I don't mean to startle you but I've wanted to see you for some time."

Rafe's heart stopped and he snapped his head towards the door. Next to the doorway was a familiar figure in black, the tips of her white wings poking up above her shoulders.

"Megan!" He leapt over to her, stopping short a pace away.

She smiled sadly. "I wanted to see you earlier but didn't know what to say. I'm... I'm sorry about your friend Evie."

His moment of elevation was brought crashing down, back to earth. He sighed. "It's been hard you know, so very hard. She was at school with me but I never really knew her until I joined the Grey Guardians."

Megan reached a hand out onto his shoulder. "I've never known loss of a close friend like you have. My mother though, she lost my father when I was very young, and I still see the pain in her face."

Rafe hadn't known about her father before and didn't know what to say, so Rafe resorted to pursing his lips and giving a brief nod.

"I hope it's not an inappropriate time but as we're on the same side, I could do with your help, and I was hoping you could do with the distraction?" One of Megan's eyebrows arched.

Rafe smiled. "I really could do with the distraction, what is it you need?"

"My mother is trying to recruit Angelic Order Oaken and Galad, and we could do with your help."

"What can I do?" A tinge of excitement creeped in.

"Your testimony of what happened in the timeline is proof that we need to come together, and your presence will demonstrate we are building a coalition. The Angelic Orders know they cannot win this battle by themselves, if they know we are building our forces up with alliances, they will side with us. While the Grey Guardians are now few in number and perhaps weak, there are not many ways to enter and watch the timeline without a Grey Guardian. So, you are a powerful ally."

Something occurred to Rafe. "But you entered the timeline."

Megan's mouth twitched at the corners. "Yes, I did. And no one must ever know that, do you understand?"

"Yes. But why?"

"There are very few ways to enter the timeline. The Grey Guardians can by the grace of The Fates who are overseers of it. There are sometimes rifts in the timeline which someone can enter, though I have never seen one of these myself. There are also some items, or artefacts which have the power to enable the holder to slip into the timeline for a short period. My family hold one such item. They are very rare and very sought after, for obvious reasons. Quite often, anyone found in possession of one is hunted for its power. My family have kept such an artefact hidden and used it sparingly." Her eyes pierced into his.

"How did your family come by the artefact?"

"My mother told me once that my father was given it as a gift from one of his closest friends before he died, I never found out who it was. If the other Angelic Orders knew we held such an item, they would turn against us, thinking we held too much power. So, you must swear to keep this knowledge a secret?"

"Of course," Rafe said.

"I am serious."

"I know. I know," Rafe pleaded more insistently.

"Good." She almost sighed with relief. "So, let's get going."

Chapter Three

Together they transcended to Castle Arndell. Megan held Rafe's arm as the Castle Gates appeared before them.

"It always gets me that does." Megan sounded a little breathless.

"What do you mean?"

"I've only ever transcended twice, both to go back in time and each time it's still breathtaking."

Rafe frowned at that, as he knew she'd visited himself and Evie in the tavern during their mission to protect Heracles. When had she entered the timeline previously? "You should probably try and see if your artefact can move you in the same timeline as well as go back."

"Good idea," Megan said, sounding a little surprised.

"What are we doing here anyway, I thought we were meeting other Angelic Orders?"

"We are however we can't just arrive by ourselves. There are procedures, so we must arrive with the rest of the party from Angelic Order Arndell."

Megan walked to the same postern game that Rafe had entered only a few weeks ago. Memories of Evie trickled through, and he eyed the ground as he walked through the doorway which had opened at Megan's touch.

They passed the guard who nodded to them. The corridors they treaded through were the same as his last visit, except there were more angels in the corridors, all walking furiously with purpose. Some carried materials around, others looked at lists and each time Megan passed, they all stopped and allowed her to pass.

"It's good you're here." Megan broke the silence, to which Rafe had been filling with thoughts from when he was here last with Evie. "You'll hear things that not many are privy to, and you may learn of something which may help you over the next few months. After what happened to Zeus, I imagine there will be more attacks on the timeline."

"I've not had contact with anyone from the shadow world since I left. What's been happening, have they found Zeus?" Rafe asked.

She sighed. "No. From what we know, he just vanished into thin air right before the eyes of other angels during a meeting. The hysteria afterwards left everyone in shock. HOG called a special meeting, where tempers were frayed and blame pointed in all directions until one stood up and said the elephant in the room. That someone, or something, had the Book of Sorothir. When this was announced, you should have seen the room, it was deadly silent. The Fates spoke as well, declaring that there had been increased attacks on the timeline, and a recruitment drive was in place to find more Grey Guardians to protect it, though it would take time. They also reported that Heracles' timeline had been breached." They'd reached the door to the throne room now but Megan waited to enter. "Most worryingly though, there was a vote to oust the Triumvirate. Thankfully, it failed."

"I thought that the rulers of HOG were determined by who was most worshipped on earth?"

"It is but in exceptional circumstances, the leader can be replaced by a committee of gods. No one knows where Zeus is or what happened to him. The gods are on edge, while the shadow world are making louder noises, they can sense that HOG's power could be on the wane. If they find out that the Book of Sorothir has been found and used, they may feel brave enough to throw off the authority of HOG. There will be a civil war and again many friends will die. So, it is important that we find and stop whoever stole my mother's part of the book. There are two other parts to the book, if the same thing goes into the timeline, you might be the only one able to catch and stop them from doing any more damage."

Rafe's mind buzzed with everything she had said, and for the first time, he also felt the weight of guilt from Evie being hurt so badly because of him. He'd wanted to make a difference in his life, but the burning desire to avenge Evie, now also grew inside him every day.

Megan pushed the door open and before him lay a contingent of Angel warriors led by Falic, clad in dark blue leather armour around his waist and steel shoulder guards, ready for battle. Silevaith wore black leather armour, no metal on show. Perhaps it was hidden in the fabrics. Arabor stood on the dais next to her, wearing a long white and black jacket. As they walked, the door hinges creaked, and they all turned.

The walk felt as though it took forever with their gazes burning into him.

"Welcome, Grey Guardian. I was beginning to think you wouldn't come." Rafe cocked an eye, unsure how he had offended Silevaith. "Now that we are all here, we should leave immediately so we do not offend our hosts."

"Don't worry about my mother," Megan said, reading Rafe's thoughts. "Although she didn't want you to come at first, I insisted. So, stay close to me, as I have sworn on my honour you would be no trouble."

"Don't worry I intend to stick to your side at all times. However sometimes, trouble finds me," Rafe said.

"This way." Her arm extended in the direction he was to go.

As the group walked through a series of doors, they came to a cobbled courtyard. There, the angels leapt into the sky, one by one, their stark white wings spreading out into the sky. It really was the most magical moment he had ever seen, and he couldn't help but leave his mouth agape.

"Why are you looking like that?" Megan asked.

"I've never seen an angel fly before. It's so graceful."

Megan smiled ruefully. "Well, you'll have to get used to it."

"How are we getting to wherever we are going?" Rafe rubbed the back of his head. "I can't fly, and you can't carry me."

"You're going to portal us there." Megan interlocked her arm into Rafe's and slid up close, which sent tingles up Rafe's body. Feeling the hard muscles through her clothes, he'd never realised how well built she was until then.

He coughed to clear his throat. "So where to?"

"To Oaken Wood. Where Angelic Order Oaken reside and Order Galad are meeting us also."

"Okay then." Rafe closed his eyes, pierced the fabric of time with his hands and opened up a hole. With Megan still holding onto Rafe, together they stepped through.

They appeared in a wooded area, surrounded by tall conifers that blocked out the sun. Beneath their feet, a layer of pines acted as a path. Megan crouched down and grabbed a handful of pines in her hand and let them fall between her fingers, watching as they fell to the ground.

It was a strange thing to do, and when Megan caught his eye, she stood and turned her face away so he couldn't see it. "You, okay?"

"Yes."

Rafe thought he saw her wipe her face.

"Just an old story my mum used to tell me. Let's go," she said rather more briskly than Rafe thought necessary.

They walked through the forest following the path of pines. It wasn't long before a large mound came into view. To the naked eye, it appeared to be two or three stories high and as wide as a sports stadium. Wild grass covered the top, but there were no trees on it except for a large oak tree at the highest point, which reached for the sky.

Even as they got close to the mound, no one challenged them. When they neared the mound, it felt as though they passed through a forcefield and once that had happened, he could now make out eight guards standing outside a cave entrance at the base of the hill. He blinked to make sure they were real.

"Who are they?" Rafe glanced sideways at Megan.

"The one dressed more ornately is Sonta Oaken, Brother to Arch Bultice. The man next to him is his son and Captain of the Guard Derys Oaken."

"I mean... they weren't there before," Rafe said aware of the timidness in his voice.

"They were, but there is a protective glamour around their home, like we do at Castle Arndell. It's so that mortals don't accidentally stumble upon it."

They walked up to the group who stood at the entrance of the cave. Butterflies fluttered in Rafe's stomach. The hard stares from Oaken Angels bore into him. He didn't mind admitting he found every angel intimidating.

"Where's your mother and her guard?" One called up, his hair wayward and orange.

"They won't be far behind; Oaken Wood is our closest neighbour out of all the Angelic Orders so it won't take them long to get here."

"How did you get here first then?" the orange haired angel asked in a mocking tone.

Rafe was unsure whether she would reveal his identity or not, but they would surely find out sooner or later given his lack of wings.

"We'll race one day and see if you can best me at flying if you like?" she teased.

Rafe was relieved that most of the stares were aimed at Megan. Whenever she entered a room, she had that uncanny talent of holding her audience captive. A quality that she shared with her mother but not something he had noticed with Arabor, her brother.

"Sonta." Megan was now stood in front of the man with wild blonde hair, her head from the neck dipped as a sign of respect.

"Megan." His smile full of warmth. "Every day you look more and more like your father."

"Megan." A younger angel with a beaming smile stepped forward, he had the same colour hair as Sonta but that's where the similarities ended, as not a single strand of hair was out of place as it fell to his shoulders. "Why are Arndell always late?" Their host smirked playfully.

"Derys!" She reached out a hand affectionately and rested it in his arm.

Derys put his hand over the top of hers, Rafe suspected that if their meeting was not of an official capacity they would probably be embracing at this point.

Rafe noted that Sonta rolled his eyes.

Derys was in stark contrast to Megan. Where she had dark hair cut above her shoulders, he was fair with shoulder length hair and broad in the chest.

Rafe looked over at Sonta and to his surprise, he found Sonta was staring right at him, for how long he had been doing so he hadn't noticed.

"And who have we here?" Sonta asked.

Rafe cast a sideways glance at Megan, hoping she would say something. When she didn't, he knew he had nowhere to hide.

"I'm Rafe," his voice sounding hollow as he spoke. He tried clearing it but the butterflies in his stomach were still there. Angels were all powerful as far as he was concerned, but what worried him most, was the fact that he'd only met one who wasn't hostile towards him so far.

Sonta raised his eyebrow, and even Derys stopped joking with Megan to listen in.

"Well, that's a turn up for the books, we don't see many of you around." He started scratching his chin and searching behind him through the cave. "This could be interesting. Are you here as Megan's guest?"

"He is." Megan confirmed with a little more punch than Rafe.

"Make sure you don't wonder off and stick with Megan," Sonta said.

Rafe didn't like the sound of this. "How come? Am I in danger?"

"No not at all, it's just grizzled old Grainne." Pointing his thumb behind him towards the entrance of the cave.

"Arch Grainne?" Megan queried.

"Well, he was let down by one a while ago, I don't know the full story but ever since then, he has had little... patience for them, shall we say." Sonta eyed Rafe.

"I'd forgotten about that." Megan giving Rafe a sympathetic face. "Sorry Rafe." Megan shrugged her shoulders.

Rafe couldn't help swallowing.

An awkward silence ensued as Rafe waited to see what else was said. "Ah, best we leave it now and save it for another day. Here comes your mother." Sonta said looking past them.

They all turned in unison to see Silevaith lead their group of Arndell Angels through the trees, mostly clad in variants of black or dark blue, except Arabor who had black and white. Behind Silevaith, came Falic and Arabor, then the contingent of Arndell warriors who were their guard. When the group arrived, it was Sonta's turn to bow at the neck.

"Archess. Welcome."

"Sonta." She smiled. "It has been a long-time old friend." She reached out an arm

onto his shoulder and gave it a gentle squeeze. It seemed a thousand things were said between them in that look. Before their moment lingered more than was deemed appropriate, she let go. "Shall we?"

"This way," Sonta led the way with Silevaith next to him. Then followed Arabor and what must have been a senior Oaken warrior who had black hair, a grizzled face, and a twin goatee beard with a silver ring that joined them at the bottom. After them was Megan and himself, alongside another Oaken warrior. Behind him was Falic and the rest of the Arndell contingent. As they walked into the tunnel, wall sconces were spaced evenly apart lighting the way, along the mud and root filled passageway.

The party moved along silently and occasionally passed other angels in the passageways, they all stopped to give a courtesy nod towards the visiting delegation. Rafe didn't dare speak, taking everything in and feeling like an intruder. He knew he stuck out.

Rubbing his clammy hands together, he took in the walls and flooring of this mythical place. Where Castle Arndell was a medieval castle, you never felt like it was run down. Oaken Wood felt earthy, an Order which was at one with nature. The wood had been a far cry from the harshness of the stone at Castle Arndell, but he was as mesmerised by this place as anything else. The mound, topped by a giant oak tree, in which he was currently descending beneath could have come straight out of a fairy tale. He would have expected the cold to reach deeper into his body with each passing step, but it actually got warmer and less dirty the deeper they went.

Up ahead, Rafe could see the end of the passage which was lit by a warm glow. When he reached the end, there was a large atrium filled with warm light. On the edge, there were stone wall balconies and buildings, finished with a small oak tree in the middle. Rafe could only describe it as a small market square, except for the large doors at the far end.

As the delegation ringed the oak tree in the middle and approached the large doors, Rafe saw guards on the balconies overlooking the entrance There were other angels who were talking or trading in goods in the square, and they too all bowed their heads. Rafe had always had a fascination of fortification defences, reading how some forces were able to overcome seemingly impenetrable defences, through cunning strategies. He'd come to the realisation that there was always a way around anything, it was just a matter of unlocking the best strategy. Rafe enjoyed analysing the defences of fortifications and the one he was in now was no different.

To any attacking force that entered the Oaken dwelling, they may have thought victory was in their hands until they realised that the layout had given the Oaken forces a kill zone from the balconies overhead. It would be a blood bath. The only way through would be to either fight your way to the balconies and hope they led somewhere. Or take the large doors, which Rafe was passing now, before they could be shut, which would be near on impossible unless someone from inside the Oaken camp helped the attackers.

Passing through the fortified doorway, Rafe watched the contingent of guards as they parted to the sides. They were dressed in earthly colours of greens, browns and reds.

On the other side, Rafe followed the Arndell Angels in front as they meandered their way through doorways, made of stone and roots together. Although there were no windows, there was always plenty of light from the wall sconces.

Eventually, they reached a doorway with two guards holding spears. They stood in front of a pair of tall wooden doors, decorated with an ornate pattern in the shape of an oak tree, made out of roots. The guards pushed the door open, revealing inside a mixture of stone walls and large pillars of roots, as thick as a person, spiralling from the roof to the floor. On the wooden throne, sat an angel whose eyes could just be seen through the mad, wiry red hair and beard of who Rafe could only deduce, was Arch Bultice.

The angels within were mostly blonde or a shade of red. Unlike the Arndell Angels which were mostly dark; brown and black haired. The Oaken Angels parted like a wave at the approach of the Arndell Angels. Arch Bultice descended the steps, wrapping his arms around Silevaith in a warm embrace.

"My old friend Silevaith. Time has been kinder to you than I, I feel. You honour me," waving his arm around the hall, "and all of us, by your presence here. Come, Order Galad are waiting in my chambers." The entourage walked towards a side door, as the rest of the congregation in the hall looked on.

Rafe still did not dare break the silence. He was distinctly aware that a number of the angels cast furtive glances towards him. Some appeared confused, some shocked and one or two displeased. He tucked in tighter to Megan.

As they entered through the doorway, Rafe noticed the door was shut shortly after him. Their warrior escort waited outside. There was only Falic, Arabor, Megan, Silevaith, Rafe, Sonta and the grizzled guard with a ring in his twin goatee, that walked with Bultice. Across the room, next to a roaring fire, stood a handful of more angels. These were clad in varying colours of greys; both dark and light. Their armour looking functional and solid with little decoration.

"Arch Grainne," Silevaith greeted as she walked over. Arch Grainne had short cropped black hair, with a hint of a bearded shadow on his jaw. It wasn't his average height that stood him out from the rest but his slow deliberate movements and piercing dark eyes.

"Archess, it is good to see you." They shook hands, noticeably more professional than the welcome Bultice and Silevaith had a moment ago.

"Come all, let's sit." Arch Bultice guided them all to a table. Three chairs were around it, where each of the three leaders took their places. Rafe ensured he was one step behind Megan and one eye on Arch Grainne all the time.

"So, Silevaith, you wanted to meet, it's been sometime since the leaders of our three Angelic Orders have been alone around a table." Arch Grainne rubbed his chin as he tried to remember. "It must have been..."

"Two millennia ago, before the Battle of Pieria."

"That's right," thumping the table at the same time.

"I find it curious that the last time we met like this was before a Battle. Tell me, it's not bad news again, is it?" Bultice queried.

"It is the worst kind of news," Silevaith confirmed. Rafe noticed Grainne's eyebrows rise. "The Book of Sorothir is being put together."

An audible intake of breath could be heard around the room, then silence, like the eye of the storm. Rafe clenched his hand into fists just to release some of the tension in him.

"And how do you know of this?" Arch Bultice's voice quivering slightly.

"For a little while now, there have been breaches in the timeline by forces unknown. The most recent breach was in Heracles' timeline, after this thing left the timeline, Zeus vanished from HOG." Silevaith stared at Bultice for confirmation.

"The Oaken were there, we can testify to that," Bultice nodding his agreement.

"Some time ago, I have held in my possession part of a book that was handed to me by Sorothir."

"What!" Bultice exploded and Rafe saw Grainne squint.

Silevaith only raised a hand in silence. "I will not justify my actions for keeping this a secret in this forum, except to say that you all know why the War in the Kingdom of Heaven ended at Pieria. It was only because of Sorothir and the group of gods, angels and Shadow world creatures brought together by my husband, Darwin. And you were fully aware, that Sorothir had no intention of handing the power of that book to us in the end. Sorothir knew above anyone, that if the book fell into the wrong hands, immeasurable destruction would ensue. To be honest, I did not know of Sorothir's plan after Pieria. I had no idea that Sorothir was waiting for me as I returned to Castle Arndell with the blood of my husband still on my hands. But there Sorothir was, after I had been to see Darwin's parents, and watched them fall to the floor weeping.

"She was in my private quarters, seemingly unnoticed by anyone else in the Castle. I was handed one third of the book, to keep hidden and never to tell anyone. I have kept that book hidden ever since, not even telling my own children. You may lament me for not telling you, Arch Grainne and Arch Bultice, but I promise you this, it was not a burden I wanted. Nevertheless, that section of book I held in my possession is missing now, and whoever took it, used whatever information was in it to make Zeus disappear," Silevaith said.

"Did you ever read the book yourself, or at least the section entrusted to you?" Grainne asked.

"I tried but it was written in a strange tongue. So, whoever has the book has a means to decipher it."

"Let's ask the obvious question first, could it be possible that it is Sorothir?" Grainne

said.

Silence followed, which became so unbearable that Rafe scrunched his toes in his shoes to send shooting pains up his feet.

"Anything is a possibility. However, you knew Sorothir, and this doesn't feel like something Sorothir would do, not even under duress," Silevaith answered.

"So how do we find who is doing it? And where are the other parts of the book?"

Everyone cast an eye about.

"No one knows, leading me to the next part of this meeting. Now knowing what you do, I hope you will see how urgent it is to reach out to old friends and start building an alliance. If the enemy make a move we need to be prepared," Silevaith said.

"Agreed," Bultice answered.

"Aye," Grainne reciprocated.

"Reach out to whoever you can and I suggest we meet again in another month to evaluate our plans. As well as building an alliance, we need a second frontal attack, to prevent it coming to a war in the first place," Silevaith instructed.

"You could be chasing your tail on that and we don't know who they are, where they are or where the next parts of the book are," Bultice said.

"I agree, Silevaith, prevention of a war would be much preferable than fighting one, but where would you start?" Rafe noticed that Grainne's eyes always darted about as he spoke, calculating everyone's thoughts.

"I agree, so we should set a minimal number of resources on this but the very fact that they exist and are real, means they will leave a trail of breadcrumbs no matter how small," Silevaith said.

"So, who will track down the enemy?" Bultice puffed out his chest.

Someone stepped forward. "I will."

Rafe couldn't believe it was Megan.

"I mean, with your permission, I will track them down," Megan said.

Silevaith raised an eyebrow in question.

"And what makes you think that you will be able to do it?" Grainne's questioned deadpan.

"Because I believe there is one person who has met the very thing tracking down the book. They know what he looks like and they were the last person to see him before Zeus disappeared. The connection between the missing part of the book and Zeus vanishing are linked, that part of the book stolen from my mother must have some form of power to control a god physically."

"And who is this person that you believe saw the thing." Bultice raised his eyebrows.

Megan cast a look sideways at Rafe, after which Rafe noted that all eyes now swivelled on him, making him feel like he was in a furnace.

"Ah, I wondered when we would get to our mysterious guest. So, who are you?" Grainne said as he tapped the tips of his fingers together in a dance.

"My name," he croaked, "is Rafe Stern. I have seen and spoken to the person that has been breaching the timeline, although at the time I didn't know who he was." Rafe fingered the bracelet on his wrist.

"And where did you see him?" Grainne asked slowly.

"In the timeline," Rafe said.

Arch Grainne's smug smile dropped, and he cast a glare towards Silevaith. "You dare bring a Grey Guardian before me?"

Silevaith held a hand up. "I know, and I wouldn't expect you to like him, I for one have little care for him, however, he may prove useful. Just listen to what he has to say."

Grainne ground his teeth, then Bultice cleared his throat. "Continue," he commanded.

Rafe couldn't help but fidget with his hands. "I was on a mission to protect Heracles, as The Fates had sensed minor disturbances in the timeline. What's strange, is that he was with us," Rafe stuttering as he remembered Evie was no longer with him. "He was with me and Heracles for days. But the day I left the timeline, was the day his father, Zeus, disappeared. It was also the same day that my friend Evie was stabbed outside HOG, which I can only presume was by him. He went by the name of Cleon however I suspect that was not his real name." Rafe omitted the fact that Cleon had given him a bracelet, once worn by Grey Guardians, he didn't want to open up that pandora's box when Grainne was already suspicious of him. "The Fates sensed something small had changed in that timeline, which was so minor they don't know what it was, but whatever Cleon did, it was enough to affect Heracles' link to Zeus."

"We heard of what happened to your friend that day, some of our own Order were there and witnessed it. We hope she makes a speedy recovery."

Rafe didn't know what to say so pressing his lips together, he nodded.

This seemed good enough for Bultice. "So, now is the time for action, our enemies are moving, and they have a head start with one part of the book," he said.

Silevaith picked her moment, as though she had already rehearsed what and when she would speak. "We do not know where our enemies are, so we need to act on different fronts and reach out to the shadow world for allies. I will approach some of the shadow creatures to see if any are willing to give us an audience."

Grainne spoke next. "We should also approach the other Angelic Orders."

Bultice raised an eyebrow.

"We have nothing to lose, and while I suspect none will join us, we may uncover something," Grainne replied to Bultice's curious look.

Silevaith nodded. "You are friendlier with some of them, than I, if you could put the feelers out."

Grainne nodded.

Bultice spoke next. "We should start preparations for war, ensure our defences are strong and weapons are sharp."

"That leaves us to search for the book, if we can deny them the book then we may be able to stop the war," Silevaith interjected. "I propose that a small group led by Megan be assigned to the search. So, they can operate covertly, if they find anything we can send reinforcements."

Both Arch Grainne and Bultice nodded in agreement. "Who shall join Megan?" Bultice asked.

"I will." Everyone looked towards Dery's.

"Nemor." A tall broad guard who stood behind Arch Grainne stepped forward. His hair was cropped short, almost to the scalp, which seemed unusual for angels. His jaw was expressionless. "You will go as well."

"I would also suggest another as well," Silevaith declared to everyone's surprise. Rafe scanned the room, to see who would volunteer but the decision was already made.

"You, will go." Silevaith's eyes pierced at Rafe.

"M-me?" Rafe couldn't help but stammer.

He seemed to once again be the centre of attention as everyone stared at him, and some even took a step back as though they could catch something from him. In the corner of his vision, Arch Grainne sneered.

"The enemy are in the timeline which is a place we cannot go, it makes sense that Rafe work with us to find the book. Besides he is the only one that has seen who we are up against." Silevaith eyed Rafe without blinking. "You seem to be at the centre of this anyway, so will you accept helping us, Grey Guardian?" It was said in such a way, that it left no doubt he had no choice in the matter.

All Rafe could muster was a nod of his head and to say, "Yes, Archess."

The curl at the end of Silevaith's mouth widened, ever so slightly.

"Then we each know what needs to be done, so until the next time we meet, I bid you all farewell." She stood and led the way to the door.

The delegation was escorted by a contingent of Oaken guards as it made its way out through the warren of tunnels. When they reached open air, they were left to make their own passage to the magical boundary which marked the Oaken stronghold. Throughout, not a single word was spoken amongst the Arndell Angels.

Outside the magical boundary, in the midst of the tall tree that towered overhead, Silevaith rose with a flap of her wings. The other angels followed one by one until only Rafe was left with Megan.

"That was... intimidating," Rafe ventured.

Smiling lopsided, Megan ruffled his hair. "You did alright."

"I suspect by your mum's coolness towards me, she planned that whole thing from the start."

"My mother is very respected amongst the angels, even before my father died. My father was the heir to the Order but when he died, his parents were so overcome with grief they broke. I was told they became hollow shades of themselves. They left the Order with little warning to end their own suffering and my mother, even with two children in tow, took the reins up and steadied us. Some may even say, she has even increased our standing. As well as strong, she is cunning, which is not a trait we were renown for previously. I would rather cross Arch Bultice or Grainne than my mother."

"Talking of Grainne, why does he hate the Grey Guardians so much?"

"I don't know the details, though rumour has it that Grainne's daughter once helped a Grey Guardian, which ended in her death," Megan said solemnly.

Rafe's hand instinctively went to the bracelet on his wrist.

"Since then, he's mistrusted them. I suspect if you hadn't already confronted our foe, he'd have prohibited you from helping. His sidekick though, Nemor, will keep an eye on us for him. We better watch sour back when we're in his presence," Megan said.

"So, what do we do now?" Rafe shrugged his shoulders.

"Wait for your next mission and keep an eye on the timeline. I will work with Nemor and Derys to see what breadcrumbs there are, that lead us to the book. I'll check in with you when I can. Look after yourself." She then rose into the air, breaking through the tree canopy.

Alone again, Rafe thought. He felt an ache inside him, in the shape of Evie.

Chapter Four

Rafe was walking with his friend Rory along the street, when he spotted a particularly round shaped stone and kicked it against the wall. But before he could react, the stone bounced back and hit him in the shin.

"Argh," Rafe cried.

"What happened?" Rory questioned in a panic.

"Ah nothing," Rafe said, rubbing his shin. He hoped he wasn't bleeding.

"Buddy?" Rory stopped in his tracks but Rafe couldn't bring himself to look up. "Mate, look at me."

It had been a while since he'd looked his best friend in the eye, and when he did, he noticed his friend's ears poking out from his curly ginger hair and his freckles on his nose.

"I'm your best friend but you haven't been yourself for weeks, I'm worried about you. I'm not trying to pry but I need to understand what happened while I was away?" Rory said seriously.

Rafe didn't know what to say, so just stared at his friend searching for an answer. "I met someone while you were away, and she became a very good friend of mine."

"Okay," Rory answered slowly, with a slight smug sound to him.

"You know her, she goes to our school. Evie from our year."

Rafe noted how Rory pulled a face, which annoyed him. "What's the face for?" Rafe couldn't help but be defensive.

"Oh, I was just surprised that's all. I heard she had an accident and was in hospital."

Rory's face was sincere on closer inspection and Rafe decided to give him the benefit of the doubt. "I got to know her while you were away. We got close and..." He felt his face begin to screw up.

Rory put an arm around his shoulders.

"It's alright, mate. Don't worry about it. It'll be okay."

Rafe was relieved Rory didn't say anything more. As there was nothing anyone could say to make him feel better. "I feel like I could have done more to prevent her accident."

"But how, you weren't there, were you?" Rory said, clearly trying to find excuses but unfortunately was far from the mark.

Rafe's mouth twisted. He wanted to tell him desperately but if he revealed the truth, it could snowball and he didn't know where it would lead. Better to brush it off, Rafe deduced.

"No one gave her a chance, and I wish I'd known her for more than a few weeks. I wish I'd been nicer to her in school as well."

"You couldn't have known, mate." Rory's arm was still around Rafe's shoulder. "Thank you for telling me. I'm here, okay."

"Thanks mate," Rafe mustered.

"Anyway, let's go and play computer games," Rory suggested.

That night, Rafe pushed his food around his plate. His parents cast furtive glances at each other. They thought he couldn't see but they weren't exactly subtle. Once he had eaten his food, he asked to be excused rather than sit in silence pretending to play happy families.

In his room, he lay on his back, thinking of the time he'd been initiated into the Grey Guardian's. He remembered the metallic taste and now realised that what he had drunk was probably blood mixed in with something sweet to mask its contents. Blood seemed to carry a certain magic in this new world he had entered. Prometheus' blood had enabled Rafe to break into realms which were seemingly impenetrable, while the blood in the cup from The Fates, was probably their own. What else could blood do? Different blood must do different things depending on the owners.

Without realising, he had been fingering the leather bracelet with the strange markings on the metal plate, that now sat on his wrist. Its presence, a constant reminder to the mysteries which still needed solving. Which Grey Guardian owned it before Cleon?

Rafe began to drift off when he was suddenly jerked awake by a strange sensation of his body becoming lighter. With a blink of his eyes, the atmosphere around his body changed. He emerged into the familiar lounge of The Fates but this time the three of them were not alone.

"Rafe, my dear, welcome," Larissa said, soothing him with her gentle tones.

"Hi, guys." Rafe tried to sound buoyant while keeping one eye on the fourth person.

"Come, Rafe." Clarence ushered him to the table where cookies sat on a plate.

The guest with The Fates was slightly taller than Rafe, nodding towards her older age. She had brown wavy hair tied into a pony, which fell below her shoulders. Freckles on her nose framed an impenetrable stare, and her arms were folded.

"Rafe, it's good to see you again." Anthony's familiar gravel voice boomed across the room. "Meet Kate McNulty." Kate nodded in his direction, her eyes moving up and down, taking Rafe in. "Kate is a Grey Guardian like you." Rafe couldn't help but raise his eyebrows at this. He knew they existed but didn't think he'd get to meet one so soon. "You two will have time to get to know each other shortly but first we have to brief you on a situation which we need addressing straight away."

"If you're not up to it," Larissa intervened. Her voice always made him feel better, calm and at ease. "Then that's okay, we'd rather know." Rafe noted she had the courtesy to not mention Evie, but he knew what the implication was.

"I could do with the distraction, to be honest," he said with a little more force than he intended.

"Good," Anthony continued. "We need you both to go into the timeline to look after Jupiter's son, as we've sensed some disturbances there."

"And who is his son?" As mental images of different historical figures passed through his mind.

Kate snorted. "The demi-god Julius Caesar, of course."

Rafe noted the touch of Irish to her accent.

"What? Seriously?" Rafe said, slightly open mouthed.

Anthony interjected. "Who else could be the Son of Rome's supreme God other than the most famous Roman of all time? What do you think happens to Rome and Jupiter, if Julius Caesar doesn't conquer Gaul hey? The Roman Empire wouldn't have been near so formidable, and Jupiter's fame would have been a fraction of what it becomes."

Rafe stared at everyone across the table and saw Clarence purse his lips.

"So, when do we leave?" Rafe clapped his hands together.

"Now." Kate stood. "The world is on a knife edge, and we have no time to lose." Kate cast a look back over her shoulder. "Are you coming or what?"

Rafe pinched his eyebrows together. "Sure." Rafe felt a little tepid about the whole mission.

Kate walked towards the front door and opened it, as Rafe followed and peered over her shoulder, and could only make out blue sky. Once over the door threshold, he heard the door click behind him. He went to see if it would open, but when he spun around, it was no longer there. There was no seam or line to suggest a hint of a door existing before. Nothing surprised him anymore.

Rafe noted that despite not seeing The Fates for some time, he was shuffled in and out, with no time for pleasantries. He was starting to see their heartless side.

Surveying their surroundings, he could see they were nowhere near to HOG, which is where the door had taken him the last time. The grass was wet under the gaze of his eye, with a slight sparkle to it. Not too far away was a dark smudge, then in another direction a tall wooden palisade, albeit a lot closer. Kate was next to him, dressed in grey leathers, with a knife at her side, she was confident and menacing.

"This way," she said waving Rafe to follow towards the palisade.

"How do you know the spears behind the walls are friendly?"

"Because that's the Roman fortification. And over there..." She nodded to the dark smudge in the distance. "Is one of Gaul's armies, which the Romans are fighting. So, I suggest if you don't want to get caught between two armies, you get a move on."

Rafe quick marched behind Kate but had to occasionally skip to keep up with her brisk pace.

As they approached the wall of sharpened wood, a challenge was shouted. "Halt. Who goes there?"

"Optio. We are Prefects of the Batavian cohort, returning as ordered by Gaius Julius Caesar," Kate shouted back.

"Probably off to report to his commanding centurion," Rafe offered in a whisper.

"So, you do know something then of the Roman era and aren't completely clueless," Kate said with heavy sarcasm.

"I love Roman history. Where and when are we by the way?" Rafe felt an edge of anxiety as he spoke.

"Alesia 52 BC," Kate said with what seemed like her usual authoritative tone.

"Oh," Rafe said with his mouth wide open, as he knew of this battle and how bloody it was.

"Yes. *Oh* indeed. The Battle of Alesia in 52 BC," Kate said without even looking at Rafe.

A small doorway opened on the palisade, which Rafe hadn't even noticed until now.

Rafe and Kate walked down the defensive ditch, lined with spiked stakes. The slope back up was steeper and hard going. Rafe was breathless as he reached the doorway, it had been a while since he'd done any exercise. Catching his breath, a shadow loomed over them, it was the on-duty Optio, identifiable by the scowl.

"Anything of note out there?" the Optio questioned in a light voice.

"The same as usual." Kate waved away with her arm.

The question prompted a thought in Rafe, as to the legitimacy of women in the Roman army. He'd seen images in history books of women fighting in Celtic and Germanic armies against the Romans but not the other way around. Perhaps the Batavians were allowed them being an auxiliary force from the provinces. From what he could remember, the Batavians ended up being allies of the Romans for centuries, and were considered to be elite fighters.

Making their way through the defensive walls looming above them, another wall ran parallel a good hundred meters away. Rafe went through his knowledge of the battle of Alesia; he remembered that it was actually a battle of three armies with Vercingetorix surrounded by Julius Caesar, who in turn was surrounded by an even bigger Gaul army. So, Caesar had constructed a double palisade, one to pen and surround Vercingetorix and one facing outwards against the relief force. It was a masterstroke of engineering and military tactics by one of history's greatest generals.

"This way." Kate angled towards a line of tents.

Weaving in and out of them, men of various shapes and sizes but all wearing red tunics under armour, cooked and played games of dice or cards. After a break in the tent lines, there was a group separated. Kate walked towards them.

Here, men wore black, mixed with black furs and armour. Each eyed them as they passed and gave a nod to Kate.

In the centre was a tent with the outline of where a campfire would later be lit.

Kate entered the tent without breaking a stride.

Inside were two beds low to the ground, with a white sheet. At the bottom of each bed was a pile of clothes, with the hilt of a sword poking out the top.

"That's yours over there. Get dressed as we need to get to the command tent as soon as we can." Kate pointed towards the bed on the right as they walked in.

"Where shall I..." He paused to see if Kate could see his predicament.

"Where what? Shall you get changed?" she said with a slight condescending tone.

"Turn your back and I'll do likewise." Kate moved over to her bed and started to take her top off. "Go on then turn your back." She pointed at Rafe's new bed.

Rafe ragged the clothes and peered down at them, trying to piece together what went where. Separating them onto the bed, he could make out a black tunic with a fur collar, shoes, armour, a sword and helmet with a black plume on top.

"Hurry up, will you?" Kate called out.

Rafe risked a glance behind and saw Kate had got her tunic and armour on already.

Rafe had never been semi-naked in front of anyone before, and he didn't like it one bit. Here goes, Rafe mouthed to himself. He took his clothes off, except his underwear, and scrambled to put the Roman clothes on as fast as he could. He found it clumsy to dress himself, but suspected some of it was down to being too hasty.

Once he had put the footwear on and buckled his sword to his waist, he stood surveying himself. He thought he dressed in the uniform rather well actually.

"It's about time." Kate standing with her legs slightly apart and her fists on her hips. She was an image of some Greek hero Rafe had seen in a book once, and most definitely fit the part more than he did, Rafe noted. "Let's get going then."

They exited the tent and headed out of what Rafe deduced was the Batavian tent lines and made their way down a thoroughfare towards the largest grouping of tents. As they neared it, one tent was raised above the rest and seemed to be where the thoroughfare ended. Working their way towards it, Rafe had the feeling of wanting to vomit. The long slow walk to one of history's greatest figures made his stomach do somersaults. It was scarier than meeting Heracles.

Kate, on the other hand, walked with a swagger, a reminder of someone he'd met previously but couldn't quite place. She was slightly taller, and if he had to hazard a guess, he would say she was about eighteen years old, give or take. She wasn't slim or large but something in between. He imagined she was probably incredibly fit and lean.

Kate, who was now half a step ahead, passed a pair of golden standards which marked the boundary of the command tent. Kate didn't slow or skip a step and had clearly been in situations like this before.

Two fearsome men guarded the entrance to the large tent. Face grizzled, scared and bearded, they held spears in hand with thick arms. They nodded as the two Prefects passed into the tent.

Inside, spice sticks burned, probably to keep the stench of sweaty men at bay. But it was the rows of seated soldiers that shocked Rafe. There were a good forty of them on wooden benches.

Rafe quickly ushered close to Kate who'd found a space and perched on the end of a bench.

He took in the men around him, observing their mannerisms, trying to pick up anything that might be useful. One thing of note was the large number of helmets with red plumes.

Off to one side was a group of three men and a boy, younger than Rafe. All four wore metal breastplates adorned with patterns. The young boy, blonde, stood to the side watching.

The eldest by some margin was tall and thin with flecks of grey at the sides. His mouth curled up, but Rafe noted his eyes darting back and forth towards his colleagues, calculating and studying.

The other two were slightly younger and brown haired; one lean, athletic and boisterous as though campaigning was all he knew, the other with more weight as though this were his first. After one final laugh from the athletic member of the group, they broke apart and faced their audience.

The low buzzing noise of chatter, which Rafe had failed to notice before, now stopped, replaced with complete silence as all eyes faced forwards.

"Men. Comrades. Brothers," the tall thin man declared, commanding everyone's attention. "We have word from our scouts that an army of Gauls, four times our number, are but two nights march away to relieve the enemy we have encircled."

Rafe nearly jumped out of his seat as the men of the tent stamped their feet once in unison.

"Vercingetorix, trapped by our walls has twice as many men as us."

The bench shuddered from the stamping of feet again.

"They have thrown themselves at our walls, but they have not broken through once. Not once." A little more forceful.

Another stamp.

"Rome did not believe we could suppress the Gauls but yet we have." Vehemence crept in a little more with this statement.

Another stamp.

"No army has ever erected a double palisade."

Another stamp and this one was the loudest so far.

"After two more nights you shall fight two enemies, and then you will make history." He was almost shouting it now. "Then you take your bounty to become rich men." He finished with a growl.

The tent erupted into a chorus of stamping.

The man at the front, flanked by his associates, soaked in the noise until finally he waved it down.

"Brutus has your orders." Caesar indicated a table at the side of the room with a map laid out, next to a man in a white toga. "The Batavian and Remi Auxiliary Cohorts are to report to my quarters. Dismissed."

The man turned his back and talked to his two, before taking his leave through a side flap of the tent.

An elbow barged into Rafe. He was about to protest back when he realised it was Kate.

"That's us, we're Prefects of the Batavian Auxiliary Cohort. Come on, let's go."

She shoved past, probably not intentionally as it was a snug fit with everyone crammed in.

While meandering through the groups of officers, the tent was alive with chatter. More than once, he bumped into someone and sidled away, apologising profusely.

"Pstt," Kate came close to Rafe. "Quit apologising to everyone! You're a Prefect, so you're more senior than most in this tent."

This time someone barged into him, so Rafe eyeballed the culprit but immediately regretted it and moved on. He wasn't cut out to be an officer in Rome's famous army. Having made their way across the tent, they appeared at an opening that two other officers were going through. Inside, he was surprised to see that besides Kate, four people occupied the room.

The two rough-looking officers who had just entered before him, dressed in black leathers and held their helmets, while at their waists were curved swords. The two other figures were behind a small wooden desk. The tall elder man with flecks of grey sat, while the young boy from earlier stood at his side.

Rafe stood to attention as best he could, copying Kate.

"Prefects of the Batavian and Remi Cohorts, report."

Kate went first. “Vercingetorix’s forces are behind their palisades. There is little movement, except their patrols and pickets have doubled on the west side. They don’t want us to see something in that area.”

“Thank you, Prefect. And you?” Inclining towards the other two officers.

“The enemy outside of the gates have, by my estimates, four thousand horse and a hundred thousand foot, they will be here as you said earlier, after two nights.”

“So, three times our number then and Vercingetorix with twice our number. Five to one, good odds.” He cast a sidelong look at the boy next to him. “What do you deduce?”

“The enemy will be gathering their forces on the west.” His voice croaky, on the cusp of breaking. “When the army outside of the palisade attacks us in the west, Vercingetorix will also strike in the west. Attempting a double pincer to overwhelm our forces there.”

“That’s what I have concluded as well. The enemy within may also send a feint attack. East to draw our forces away from the main attack but it’s essential we do not. We will re-enforce the west side of our palisade with the more armoured legionnaires. You, Prefects, will instruct your auxiliary units to fortify the east to drive off any feint they may throw at you. Octavian here will lead you.”

Rafe noticed the boy straightening his back, with pride or shock, he couldn’t tell which. To Octavian’s credit though, his face remained impassive at the burden of leadership which had just been bestowed on him.

“You will prepare your forces tomorrow and move off to the east the next morning for battle. That is all, you are dismissed.”

Outside the tent, Rafe couldn’t help but inadvertently sigh, letting his shoulders sag.

Kate cocked an eye and gave him a half smile. "Relieved to be out of there, are you?"

Rafe couldn't help but smirk. "Just a little. So, what now?"

"We do as we're ordered and we take our Cohort to the east and wait for the battle."

"But we don't have a Cohort. Do we?"

"You don't, but I do. What do you think I've been doing the last few months while you were in Ancient Greece. The rest of us have been on assignment." Rafe noticed the use of the word *us* and made a mental reminder to ask her about it later. "I've cultivated an identity here, and my Cohort are loyal down to the bone. Come on, let's introduce you to them."

They had made their way around part of the double palisade out of the Command parade square and down a narrow part of the double spiked walls. The shadows grew longer as the sun dipped down in the sky, and a few fires were being lit among the camp and walk ways.

All around, men bustled back and forwards. On one occasion, they passed a column of men in the red tunics, silver armour and the rectangle shields of Roman legionnaires. At the head was a man in ornate armour, flanked by courtiers. After them, came a man holding a tall pole with four large circular pendants on. The men behind marched four abreast, some with scars and all with unsmiling faces. This was a veteran force, well-seasoned and completely aware of what battle would bring. As the lines passed, they were interspersed with the centurions and their plumed helmets. Rafe knew these were the heartbeat and soul of each legion. As the line went on, Rafe passed the time counting twenty rows for every centurion he passed. centurion followed by men, repeated over and over. This must be one of the legions being moved into position for the battle tomorrow. After the last of the men passed them by, they were once again able to command the centre of the path of now trodden mud. Rounding a final corner, they came to a cluster of tents. At the entrance of this parade area, a guard challenged them, the first of the evening to stop them. He didn't wear the red tunic and armour of the legions, but the same black tunic and fur that Rafe wore.

"I didn't spot you there Prefect. My apologies," said the soldier.

"Don't apologise, Optio Lucia. You were ordered to challenge anyone attempting to enter our camp, and you did just that. You can't be too careful of spies around here." Clapped him on the shoulder, as she passed. "Keep up the good work soldier."

Rafe noticed from the corner of his eye the guard watching him pass. The man had a light shade of beard on his face, but the most distinguishing feature was the deep gash of scar tissue across the bridge of his nose, making Rafe feel like a boy amongst men.

Approaching a campfire at the centre of the tents, Rafe noticed six men in the same black fur tunics as Optio Lucia. One man at the far end with no hair and few teeth to go with it, said something that the other five thought was funny and all broke into loud laughter. As Kate entered the firelight, all five stood hurriedly.

"Prefect," the bald headed one said.

Rafe watched Kate and the man eyeball each other. What was going on?

Then both Kate and the bald man smiled, sniggering as they held out their arms and embraced forearms.

"Centurion Tigris, I hope you saved me and Prefect Rafe some mutton," Kate said with a smile.

"The best cuts, Prefect." As she weaved her way through to the pot hung over the crackling campfire, she clapped the other five men on the shoulder as she passed them. Each nodded their respects to their commander.

Rafe stood in awe at how these men had unflinching respect for Kate. These were grown, seasoned warriors, who undoubtedly had faced numerous perils, and they treated Kate as one of their own. How had she done that?

"Come, Rafe." Waving Rafe to join her.

Rafe watched each step he took, ensuring he did not fall. It would be typical of him to lose his footing in front of men he would be fighting alongside.

"Centurion's. This is Prefect Rafe, recently assigned to us." She held an outstretched hand to each centurion as she introduced each one. "Centurion Tigris commands my first century. Then there is Centurions Tarracus, Paulis, Gallac, Hurix and Felix." He couldn't make out all of their features in the fading light but for Tigris, the majority had fair hair.

Clearing his throat gently, so as not to be noticed, Rafe raised his voice. "Centurions! It is an honour to stand with you." He wasn't sure if it was the right thing to say but it sounded macho enough to him.

"He'll do, Prefect," Tigris said nodding his approval to Kate.

All the men around the campfire raised their jugs and cheered.

After the noise died down, Kate addressed her officers. "Right, listen up, lads. Our esteemed Julius Caesar, has ordered the legions to reenforce the west where they believe the main attack will occur. Us and the other auxiliary units are to hold the east from any feints they may throw at us. We can expect battle to commence in two sleeps from now, so tomorrow, get everything prepared, weapons sharpened and armour cleaned, then in the early streaks of grey the following day, we are to form up and wait for Octavian to lead us to battle. Is that understood?"

"Aye," someone said followed by a few murmurs of approval.

"Good, enjoy the rest of the mutton, lads," Kate said. "Come, Prefect." Kate nudged Rafe while holding two small bowls of brown liquid. She led him to a tent and kicked open the muddy flap of her tent. He sat on his bed.

"So, what do you think?" Kate handed him a bowl.

Where did Rafe start, he wondered.

"How do those centurions know you so well? I mean they respect you so much, how did that happen?" He took a mouthful of soup with a wooden spoon afterwards. "Ah, that's hot."

"I've been here for a while now. Months, in fact." She blew on her spoon, the steam rising off it.

Rafe took another sip off his spoon but this time he was prepared for the heat.

"When The Fates first spotted something happening in the timeline, I was assigned to watch Julius Caesar and Octavian."

He looked up at this. "How come?"

"Normally, The Fates know where to send us but these recent distortions in the timeline spooked them. Even Larissa seemed nervous. So, they scattered us across history, to embed ourselves close to important figures and wait to see if anyone turns up. I hadn't left this place until Zeus disappeared." She moved a loose strand of hair that had fallen into her bowl of food. "So, what happened in HOG that day?"

Kate took another mouthful.

There was only one thing he could think of, which was the image of Evie motionless and bloodied. He hadn't realised how long he had been silent for until Kate prompted him.

"Tell me," Kate commanded, leaving little choice but to adhere.

"We were going to HOG to see Zeus, when all hell broke loose. I didn't see it coming, no one saw anything. There was a blur, a flash of light reflected off metal." He could picture himself there now, he hadn't done this in a long time, it had been too painful before. He saw wet dots on his lap. Wiping his eyes, he hadn't noticed the tears streaming down his face. When did that happen? "Someone threw a knife and it hit Evie. She was my friend."

Kate stood up from her bed, which creaked as the weight eased from it. She moved to sit by Rafe. "How is she now?"

Rafe just shrugged, not knowing what to say. The Fates had put her in a sleep-like state, but her body wasn't healing itself, something about the wound was stopping it. And unless her body healed itself, she would be like that forever. Or until the hospital decided to pull her life support.

Rafe took a deep intake of breath through his nose, smelling a strange scent of flowers coming from Kate.

"The Fates told me that this Cleon fellow was likely an ex-Grey Guardian," Kate said, "and he gave you a bracelet. Can you show it to me?"

Rafe pulled his sleeve up and showed her and without warning Kate grabbed his wrist and squeezed hard.

It hurt so much he gasped. "Ow!" He felt the pressure relent but only a little and she brought it up to her face. Then she did something strange by running a thumb over the markings.

Rafe fought the urge to push Kate away but wanted to find out what she had spotted. "What is it?" Rafe asked.

Throwing his wrist down and storming to her cot. She stood there with her back to him, without speaking.

"What is it?" Rafe asked again, starting to feel a little freaked out.

"I've seen a few of these before, only a Grey Guardian would have one of those."

So, it was true, Cleon was an ex-Grey Guardian, Rafe thought. But even if he had been, Kate's reaction was a bit over the top, something wasn't quite right.

A horn blared in the night and Rafe half expected to see someone burst in shouting an alarm.

"Lights out." Kate grabbed her thin bed sheet and threw it open. Pulled the leather strap of her armour lose, flung it to the ground and climbed into bed, wrapping the sheet above her head.

"Dim the candle when you go to bed,-." Kate growled.

Rafe feeling confused by her reaction, fumbled with the clasp of his own armour. When he'd carefully placed it next to his bed, he got under his covers, feeling slightly worried. Kate knows something.

Chapter Five

Rafe pried his eyes open, the air crisp but warm under his animal skin cover. He reached down to feel the hilt of his sword. Kate said to keep his weapon at hand, so ensured it had been accessible all night, just in case. But he also put his hand at the lump next to his breast, a gift more important that the sword on the floor. He glanced over at the cot next to him to see the steady rise and fall of Kate's breathing.

Swinging his feet over the bedding, his boots felt the dampness underfoot. He scratched at his side, the material of his tunic had irritated him all night. Wanting to get out of there, Rafe hastily strapped his armour on. While buckling his belt, it slipped and clattered against his sword. Rafe cursed.

"What are you doing?" Kate's groggy voice drifted over her covers.

"I'm going for a walk. I need to get out of here." Rafe picked up his belt, pulling it too tight in his haste.

"Where to?"

"I don't know. I just need some air," Rafe said.

"I'll come with you," Kate said and sat up.

"You don't need to. Why not stay in bed a little longer?" Feeling like he wanted to be away from her after last night.

"No, I will come with you. I could do with the fresh air as well," Kate insisted.

Rafe wished he could go for a walk by himself, but there was no shaking her, so he resigned himself to it. "I'll see you outside then." He trudged through the tent flap.

Outside of the tent, the cool air and bright sunshine hit him. He hadn't felt this sensation since the time he had been camping with his family, which was a long time ago. His parents had been insistent they went on those camping holidays, full of cold nights, stuffy mornings and half-cooked food over a camping stove.

He missed those days, especially the campfires, jokes and games with his mum, dad and sister. What would they have made of all this?

A shove from behind announced Kate's arrival. He'd almost forgotten she was coming. "Let's go," Kate said as she stomped off.

Following half a step behind her, he tried to put the events of last night behind him. he noticed how the auxiliaries stopped as she passed and nodded to her.

The sun was a thumbs width above the horizon and already the camp was beginning to bustle with activity. On the inside and outside ramparts, helmets of the guards extended as far as the eye could see.

Rafe allowed Kate to lead them through the camp and eventually came to a stop beside an auxiliary that was grinding a mortar and pestle.

"Optio Aulus." Kate stood with her hands in her belt.

"Prefect." Optio Aulus stood to attention.

"What's the report on our two injured?" Kate asked, waving him down.

Before he could answer, a loud braying followed in the camp somewhere, followed by a smashing noise. "What's that now! Stay here, Rafe, and get me a report on the injured, I'll be back."

Rafe stood staring at the Optio. Who in turn stared back and waited for Rafe to say something.

"So," Rafe managed to meek out. "The Prefect would like a report on the injured."

"Both men are fine and expected to make a full recovery, sir," Optio Aulus reeled out.

"Ah good. The Prefect will be happy," Rafe said in a voice which he thought a superior would use.

They stood staring at each other again, making Rafe even more uncomfortable. Spotting the mortar and pestle, he nodded towards it.

"May I, sir?" Aulus waved to the box he was using for a seat.

"Please."

Aulus sat and pulled up a spare box next to him, which Rafe took.

"What is it?" Rafe spied something green in the mixture.

"This here." Aulus twisted his hand to grind it together. "Is a herbal mixture. It's not perfect, but it's the best I can do with the limited supplies and foliage out here. Still, it works."

"What do you use it for?" Rafe asked, peering over.

"For anything you want, but in the case of this one, this is for healing," Aulus said.

Herbs for healing powers, Rafe thought, remembering some shops from his high street which sold herbal remedies. He was shocked to see it being used two thousand years ago, but then natural remedies would be the only source of ingredients. They didn't have factories in this era, to artificially make paracetamol for instance.

The grinding of the pestle continued. "None of the legions use this as they mistrust it."

"What? The use of herbs and plants?" Rafe said incredulously.

"Yes, but my tribe back home in Batavia, have learned the secrets of herbology and harnessed it for a long time. The Prefect has adopted us and is now one of us. She knows its powers of healing and she encourages us to use it. But she also knows that if the Generals or Senior Tribune found out, we could be punished. So, we keep it to ourselves," Aulus said without looking up.

Rafe wanted to know more, but he needed to win his trust. "Go on. The Prefect and I are closer than comrades, and I am curious about herbology. Please forgive my ignorance, but how did your tribe come about it?"

Aulus cast his eyes about. "Do you know where Batavia is?"

The confusion on Rafe's face must have said it all, for Aulus saved him from guessing.

"It is on the coast north of here."

Rafe tried to make a mental calculation of what sea areas were north of Gaul. He would have to look it up when he got home.

Aulus continued. "My tribe are seafarers and people from all around trade with us. An elder of my tribe who has since passed, once went on a trade mission and brought back primitive goods from lands afar but more importantly, he brought back the knowledge of using plants. Most of the tribes around us had primitive use of using local wildlife for food and for construction. However, this elder brought back knowledge of how to use plants to ease pain and increase healing. The elder claimed that the tribe he met on his travels, even boasted of the knowledge of how to bring someone back from the dead. And despite everything that was offered to them, they would not divulge their closest secret."

Rafe's heart skipped a beat thinking of Evie. "Who were these people?"

"Their name was only heard by our elder, who called them Tuatha De and said they wore knotted patterns on their arms."

"Tuatha De." Rafe rolled it across his tongue to see if it revealed any clues, but none came to mind.

"Yes. The elder taught us what he'd learned, and since then we have used this knowledge to help the sick and wounded."

To be fair, Rafe thought. There were plenty of highstreets and brands in his own world which used natural ingredients from plants, so why should it be any different for Aulus?

"Thank you for sharing your history with me. I enjoyed learning more about where you come from," Rafe said.

"You're welcome."

Rafe stood and took his leave, making his way to find Kate. What an interesting story Aulus had shared, Rafe mused. It might not have been a tale from the fables, but the story of a common man in ancient times carried as much weight as the legendary stories of Julius Caesar. He wished Aulus all the best.

He heard Kate before he saw her. Rounding a tent, Kate berated a Roman soldier who stood next to an upturned cart. He kept his distance until she dismissed him.

As Kate walked over, she had a face of thunder. "Gosh! The incompetence of some people." She ranted as she drew level. "How hard is it to keep control of an animal? Plus…" She lowered her voice, "it's good for morale to show the Cohort, that the legionnaires can't get away with everything." She shoulder bumped him. "So, how was Aulus? What did he say?"

"He said the two soldiers would make a recovery."

"Good. He is a whizz at healing, the best in the army. I keep getting asked by the Generals how we cure so many of our wounded, but I can't give them the truth."

Rafe nodded. "Aulus said something of them mistrusting herbology."

"They still use Greeks for their surgeons who like to hack and slash their way to recovery. However, these Batavians, they have some secrets best kept to themselves."

"Aulus told me of the way their tribe came about the knowledge of healing. He said they got it from a tribe called Tuatha De, ever heard of them?"

"Hmm, not off the top of my head but they'll be in the records somewhere when we get back. So, what did you want to do on your walk? Where were you planning on heading?" Kate asked.

"I don't know really, I just wanted to get some air, it's a lot to take in being here. I mean, we're in Ancient Rome and this is only my second time being in the timeline."

"You handled the Heracles case well though. I mean, I know Zeus went missing in the end but you kept Heracles alive at least." Kate shrugged.

It seemed to Rafe a funny sort of compliment, especially after last night. "So, what happens in this timeline?" Rafe ventured.

"Well, Vercingetorix will attack tomorrow. The fight will be brutal and bloody and there are a lot of casualties but the Romans ultimately win. Their construction of the double palisade was an incredible engineering feat." Sweeping her arm across their path to highlight the Roman walls.

The Romans had created a wooden wall to pen in Vercingetorix within a village, but also a wall on the outside to prevent any relief forces aiding the Gaul. Every so often, a tower pierced the sky, soldiers atop keeping watch on the horizon on both sides of their fortification. Walking through the camp, he could see men busy at work; cleaning kit, sharpening weapons and playing games with dice. A trumpet at one time on their walk sounded, and they paused to watch a legion of soldiers stomping off towards one of the walls. Probably relieving those that guarded them.

"So," Rafe said looking for small talk to fill the void. "What is your favourite era you've visited?"

"Now that's a tricky question," Kate admitted. "There are so many good ones but I adore walking Victorian London. The sights, clothes, the people, there's something... romantic about it."

That last bit took him by surprise. He'd never have expected the word romantic to come out of Kate's mouth.

She continued, "I can still smell fresh bread filling the streets form the bakery. There was less hustle and bustle in that period, it was very peaceful."

"Sounds nice," Rafe said sarcastically. "I don't know what my favourite period would be in all honesty. Greece was pretty epic, and I can't really judge Roman times by this battle field."

They'd walked sometime chatting like this, back and forth, revealing a side of Kate which Rafe would never have expected only a few hours ago.

"So, what's your story then, Kate?" Rafe said gingerly.

"What's my story? Well, I was recruited when I was young..." Kate started.

"I mean back home," Rafe interjected. "Tell me about your home."

"Oh gosh. I live in New York with my mum, dad and two older sisters and younger brother."

"Wow, that's a crowded house."

"Yeah, but I love it, my siblings are great. Susie is the eldest, she is amazing at violin, Lottie is next and she is the politest, nicest person you've ever met. She's friends with literally everyone she meets. And my younger brother, well he's still young but a complete whizz at computers and maths. He'll work for some tech giant when he's older."

"What about you though? What did you like before all of this?" Rafe nodded at the path in front of them.

"I loved sport, especially running and volleyball."

"So, do your family know what you do now? With the Grey Guardians?"

"Are you kidding! None of our families know what we do. If we told them, do you think they would really believe us? No, they don't know anything. When The Fates came knocking in my dreams, I knew I was destined to do something special, this was my calling. How about you? What was it like before they recruited you?" Kate asked.

He sensed her eyes raking him over and undoubtedly thinking, '*Why had The Fates chosen someone overweight and lacking in courage?*'

"I don't know why they picked me to be honest, as I don't think I'm the usual type of Grey Guardian." He watched her mouth for any confirmation of the statement, but to her credit, she kept her mouth firmly pressed together. "But when they came calling, I was scared, I won't lie but I needed something to get out of my downward spiral, you know?"

"What do you mean?" Kate said, she'd stopped in the middle of the path to face him, hair tied up and hands on hips, a picture of defiance.

"I'm not the fittest guy, I know, I'm not stupid but it seems people I go to school with want to remind me constantly." The chanting of *big big Rafe, big big Rafe* echoed quietly somewhere in his head and wished he had a switch to mute the words. "While you were destined for greater things, I was not, I just want my life to mean something other than constantly being reminded of how I look." He patted his stomach. While in Greece, he had lost some weight, but he knew his moping around and comfort eating had put it back on.

They'd reached the end of their tent lines and a group of men to one side were having a drink and some bread. Another pair close by were rolling dice on a barrel. Gambling even this early in the morning, Rafe mused. Leaning against the inner palisade was a makeshift counter and tent that seemed familiar.

"Mornin' fellas," a Scottish voice called out to passing soldiers. "Can I interest ya in some meat pie. No? Suit ya selves then. Ah what do we 'ave here then?"

"Hello Sherlock," Kate greeted him warmly. "How's the camp been while I was away?"

"Not so bad, I made a fair trade. I suppose when all ya 'ave ta eat is stale bread, cheese and dried meat, one of me delicacies is like 'eaven to these lot. And master Rafe, it's great to see ya still alive and ave ya 'ead on ya shoulders. That Hydra was a nasty thing, I came to get ya soon after but ya 'ad gone," Sherlock said in his thick accent.

"Evie and I had gone through a portal to the Underworld, so we must have just missed you," Rafe offered.

Sherlock whistled. "Brave souls goin' there, ya are. And I'm sorry 'bout Evie, me lad. I 'eard wha' happened, not nice business tha'. Not nice at all." Sherlock swept a strand of loose greasy hair back with one of his big hands.

"She's in hospital at the moment but I'm going to figure out how to get her back," Rafe said.

"I do hope so, lad. While ya are 'ere, can I interest either of ya in a meat pie? If the lads see their seniors buyin' it, it'd help drum up extra custom for me." Sherlock pleaded "please."

"What's in it?" Kate queried, nose turned up.

"Hare and potato. Caught it me self this mornin' before those Gauls woke up an' snatched 'em." Sherlock barking out a laugh, his round stomach bouncing up and down at the same time.

"I think I'll pass," Kate said with her nose wrinkled.

"You know what, Sherlock. For Evie's sake, I'll take one." Rafe beamed.

"Bless ya lad." Sherlock handed a pie over, with his bare hands.

Rafe took it, trying to take his mind off asking whether Sherlock had washed his hands first. The pie still felt a little warm in his hands and made his mouth water a little.

"I, errr, don't have any money on me, can I give you some when I get back home?" Rafe thought he sounded a bit sheepish.

"No problem, lad. I'll start a tab and ya can settle it when I see ya next then," Sherlock said.

"Thanks, Sherlock." Rafe took a bite. He was half expecting to crunch on some bone or gristle, but to his surprise, it actually tasted all right. He just hoped it was hare in there and not something untoward.

"We'd better get going Sherlock, we have to get the men on parade soon," Kate suggested, pulling a face at the pie in Rafe's hands.

"Right ya are Prefects," Sherlock acknowledged with a wink.

As they walked away, the pair of men who had been playing dice, stood up to take a look at what Rafe was eating.

"What's it like, sir?" one asked who had his front teeth missing.

With half a mouthful, Rafe said, "It's delicious! Best pie outside of Rome."

"Excellent." Both men strode over to Sherlock's stall, rubbing their hands together. Rafe made a mental note that he may owe Sherlock for the pie but Sherlock would owe him for marketing the food.

Chapter Six

The rest of the day he did drills, marching and inspecting. When the sun was three quarters over the sky, they sat on a bench with the other centurions. After a hard day's work, it was nice to relax and he shuffled up to Kate and plucked up the courage to ask what he'd wanted to know ever since he got there.

"Kate?"

"Yes?" She arched a questioning eyebrow.

"I was wondering, would you sort of spar with me? Train me a bit?" Rafe asked a little sheepishly.

"Why?"

"Well, I've not had much training, and something tells me I'm going to need it," Rafe said while fidgeting with a loose bit of wood on the seat.

"Alright then, show me what you've got." She stood up, dusting herself down.

"What. Here?" Rafe looked over at the other centurions close by.

"Well, there's no time like the present," Kate answered as she backed a few metres' away.

"I didn't mean in front of the centurions," he hissed, so no one would overhear.

"Ah, don't worry about them." Kate shouted to Tigris, who was deep in conversation with Paulis, "you don't mind us training, do you?"

"No, Prefect, you carry on." Tigris turned back to is conversation.

"I'll watch though," Filia said and walked over to the bench Rafe had just vacated.

Rafe didn't feel overly comfortable about being watched but he had no choice but to pick up a spear and shield from a pile close by and then assume a defensive position.

"Hmm, interesting stance. Nicely balanced though." She walked around him. "So, you've had some training I can see."

"A little but only with a sword and shield, not with a spear." Rafe felt a little guilty, but he dared not tell her who gave him his initial training.

"Well, a spear is deadly when used right." Rafe knew that, he'd been easily defeated when sparring with Cleon on the *Mynach*. "However we don't want to kill each other so let's use the blunt ends." Rafe mimicked Kate and switched the point to behind him, so the blunt part of the spear was in front.

Kate took her position opposite.

"The spear can be used in many ways, so I'll show you some of the moves and what they are for."

Rafe saw a blur and before he realised what had happened, his shield had tilted sideways exposing his side.

"The spear can be used to tilt an opponent's shield, exposing them so another can make the killing blow." She nodded to Filia, who ambled over and mimicked an attack on Rafe's exposed side. Filia slapped him on the back afterwards and laughed.

"Let's start again," Kate declared. "It can also be used to keep the enemy at bay." She jabbed towards him. "And to blind the enemy." She feinted a jab at his face, and he couldn't help but blink. Rafe raised his shield to protect himself and stumbled backwards. He was sure she'd come towards him with the spear. He tentatively lowered his shield but was shocked to see Kate was not in front of him. In the corner of his eye, he saw her standing with a smug look on her face.

"Don't be so hard on yourself." She tapped the spear against her foot. "While the spike at the end is usually the deadly part, the whole of the spear is actually a weapon. Filia, if you please." She indicated a space in front of her.

"Now, Prefect, go easy on me, okay." Filia wasn't smiling now as he held his hand open to Rafe, who shook off the shield from his arm, held in place by leather straps, and handed it to Filia.

Without a moment's hesitation, Kate launched a series of spear thrusts which swirled in the air. One strike clattering against the shield of Filia who took a step back. Kate didn't let up and thrust forward. Filia spun out of the way, but he wasn't fast enough as Kate tracked Filia and followed up with an overhead cut. It smashed his shield downwards, driving into the ground and pulling Filia down onto one knee. Filia smiled as he eyed the length of the spear aimed at him.

"Thank you, Filia." Kate held an arm out, which Filia took and pulled himself to his feet. "I hope that was gentle enough?"

"I've had worse." Filia smirked as he patted his trousers down. When Filia passed Rafe, he leant in and said in a hushed tone. "No one can best her, she's got a talent for fighting."

"What is the key to fighting someone with a spear?" Kate's spear pointed down into the ground.

"To get inside the weapon?" Rafe meekly answered.

"Yes! If you rush me now, then my weapon's effectiveness diminishes. Try it." Kate raising her spear at Rafe.

Lifting his shield, Rafe jogged forwards, the spear glanced to the side.

"Good," Kate declared. "When we're in formation, it's important that the shields are locked together, and a wall of spike's are presented to the enemy. The row behind raises their spears overhead like this." She demonstrated with the spear being held like a javelin thrower. "It provides an unappealing target for the enemy, and any that get in around the spear will have other spears raining down on them. Let's practice fighting now."

Kate and Rafe sparred back and forward, and after a few minutes, he was sweating and breathing heavily, having forgotten how heavy weapons and shields were. Despite his fatigue, Rafe clenched his teeth and kept going.

He knew his arms were weak, and it wasn't long before his spear started dipping, and Kate started getting inside his guard. If he was honest, he preferred the sword, it was less clunky and most important of all to him, it weighed less. He'd like to have said he was there for hours practicing, but he knew he wasn't.

"Stop," Rafe requested, clutching his side.

"You need to practice more." Kate instructed him without a hitch in her breathing.

"I... know," Rafe retorted back in between gasps of breath. If he didn't sit, he would faint, so having seen a stool close by he stumbled to it and plonked his bottom on it.

"The other Grey Guardians are fitter than you," Kate said, making Rafe wince a little. Most of the world was, Rafe thought, but she didn't need to be so blunt about it. "Sisi is quick, Anika is clever and Dax is fearless. What have you got? Are you a genius of sorts?"

"Not really," Rafe said quietly as he tried to tame his breathing. If he was honest, he had no idea why The Fates even selected him.

His breathing started to ease, but the fabric of his tunic agitated him, so he repositioned it.

"Well then, you need to lose some weight, otherwise you'll end up a corpse," Kate said unflinchingly.

At that point, something snapped in Rafe. "I KNOW! I don't need you rubbing it in my face, alright!"

Rafe half expected Kate to hit him in the face as she stood over him, impassive.

"Again." She thrust her spear against the ground to make her point ram home.

Rafe pushed himself up begrudgingly and made his way over to where she stood waiting.

Kate had her legs braced, with her shield and spear pointing to the front.

He stood and stamped his feet, legs starting to seize up. As he took the few steps to assume his position, he noticed that all the centurions hadn't spoken for a while. And to Rafe's horror, they were all staring at him. Some sat, some stood but they all watched, no eating or drinking, their focus was purely on them.

What had he been taught before, not by Kate but by Heracles and Cleon? He didn't have a sword, he had a spear, which he was useless at, and he had a shield. Cleon had shown him how a shield could be used as a weapon. What else? Sliding his left foot on the floor, imitating that he was bracing his feet, he felt the earth move. The constant trampling of nailed boots, meant there was no grass and the light rain from the previous day had softened the earth. Perhaps he could use it to his advantage. Using the shield to obstruct Kate's view, Rafe bent down as though to tighten his footwear and grabbed a clump of earth.

Casting a gaze up, Kate still stood still as a statue. "Hurry up," she beckoned.

There was only one thing for it, placing the earth in his right hand, which was only loosely holding the spear, he stood up facing her.

When he was set in position, Kate came at him with speed. Feinting her spear one way, she kicked out, connecting with his shield. Rafe took a few steps back. Without a moment's hesitation, Kate jabbed at his shield. She was quicker and stronger than him, that much was obvious to everyone. Which meant he had to be more like Anika, he had to be clever and cunning.

Rafe dipped his spear head down, feigning tiredness.

Seeing his spear dip, Kate took the bait and arced her spear sideways and clattered it against Rafe's shield. She pulled back again for another but this time to back hand onto Rafe's spear. Rafe did not block it, instead, he let his spear go, forcing Kate to stumble. Rafe took the only opportunity he knew he would have and charged forward. A roar screamed from him. Rafe's shoulder connected with something but not really knowing what as his eyes were half closed. He felt Kate move backwards, skidding on the floor. He'd nearly pushed her to the ground.

Rafe's euphoria was short lived as Kate spun out of his charge. Rafe tried to mimic her as quick as he could and flung the earth from his hand into her face. She grappled at her face. "Arghh, what have you done!" Kate yelled.

Although Rafe was now spearless, he eyed his shield. Gritting his teeth and gripping the straps of his shield tightly, he pushed his body and arm into the back of the shield and rammed forwards.

When the shield connected, it momentarily stopped, jarring Rafe's arm.

That hurt, he thought, but he kept up the pressure and barged forwards again. This time, he felt himself going over and he braced himself for impact, landing on top of Kate. She pushed him off, so he slid to the floor with his arm still in the shield strap, it twisted underneath him. He tried to wrestle it free but before he could do anything, his vision went black and his head pounded. All he could hear was ringing.

"Argh!" he shouted. Rafe felt himself starting to panic and finally wriggled his hand from the shield and pried his helmet off. Above him, a panting Kate stood with her spear by her side.

Standing was an effort, as he clambered up feeling tender all over. He eyed the centurions, of which Paulis and Tigris stood open mouthed, their jugs of drink halfway to their mouths.

Rafe could feel phlegm in his mouth and swallowed it down, making him heave. He leaned to one side, hand on hip holding his stitch in place. He really hoped she didn't want to go again and debated on the merits of begging for mercy, if she insisted.

"Good, you're not totally dead inside then." Kate made her way to a jar and poured herself a drink.

To Rafe's relief, Filia came over. He picked up Rafe's shield and spear from the ground, for which Rafe was thankful for, as he didn't know if he'd be able to bend to the floor for a while.

"You deserve a drink for that." Filia winked at Rafe.

"But I lost."

"Maybe so, but I've never seen anyone get that close to besting her, our Prefect is a Shewolf. That was very clever what you did, by the way, you almost had her with the mud. I did wonder why you were a Prefect but now I know, you're a cunning one."

As Rafe shuffled over to the group of centurions, they all began to cheer and clapped Kate and Rafe on the back. Someone thrust a drink in his hand, which he took and drank a large swig of. It tasted of vinegar and burnt his throat but he could feel the aches in his body ebbing. Kate came over and raised her own cup to him. As simple as that, their moment of conflict was forgotten, and he bumped his cup into hers before setting his cup on the side.

He stayed for a little longer and listened to their stories. He couldn't help but keep watch of Kate, at how the men gravitated towards her and showed deference. But also, to see if there were any lingering feelings of anger towards him. To her credit, she didn't seem wounded by his unorthodox fighting or for him shouting at her. She had grated on him with her berating but he shouldn't have snapped. At school, when he was constantly reminded of his inadequacies, he never bit back, knowing it would only encourage more name calling.

"Right," Kate declared. "It's time to set the evening guards. Each send your Optio to my quarters, where I will give them orders for your centuries. Thank you for the drink." She placed her empty cup down.

As she walked past each man and laid a hand on their shoulder, they each nodded and mouthed a salute of "Prefect."

"Come Prefect," she commanded to Rafe. We made our way back to the tent and after a minute of awkward silence, Kate coughed. "I should not have berated you like that."

"I should not have shouted at you in front of the men either. Especially since I am used to hearing what you said, I don't know why it affected me this time."

"Perhaps you are not the person you thought you were, now that you are a Grey Guardian." She pointed to her heart. "In here, perhaps you have changed."

He hadn't really thought about that, he always thought his anger stemmed from worrying about Evie.

"Still," she continued. "It was unkind of me."

"I'm sorry too," Rafe said, feeling like a weight had been lifted.

Although he was walking side by side with Kate and couldn't quite see her face, he thought he saw a brief smile.

They reached their tent.

"I suggest you go inside and get some rest. I'm going to wait outside and set the sentry duties."

He didn't need telling twice. He didn't hear the Optio's come and go for their orders or Kate get into bed later.

Chapter Seven

He'd been restless all night, and when he finally felt as though he had fallen asleep, a voice jolted him awake.

"Prefects, it's time." Rafe could make out a familiar face poking through the tent flap.

"Thank you, Optio." Kate said, already sat up on her bed putting her armour on.

She took a sip from a flagon that she grabbed from the floor, wiped her mouth dry, and placed it back beside her bed. "Don't be too long, Rafe. It's not good form to be up after the men, gives a bad example." She strode towards the door.

Rafe reached for his armour. It felt heavier than yesterday and he had difficulty tightening the straps. When he felt ready, he exited the tent with what he knew to be feigned confidence.

He spotted Kate in a makeshift parade ring with a group of soldiers, which he hadn't seen last night. He made his way over to her.

The parade ring was only a small clearing amongst the tents, and men streamed in from all directions. The clanging of armour and weapons was the only noise, as they each ran to their formation. Rafe slowly walked to Kate, ensuring he was next to but also one step behind her. She was in command after all, Rafe thought.

Watching the men scurry like ants, it may have come across as chaos to an unobserved eye but as he watched, it was very apparent that each man knew where his final place was and it wasn't long before they formed up. There were no torches lit and the sky only had the slightest tinge of grey to it but from what he could make out, each man was equipped with a spear and oval shield decorated with a swirling pattern. This was in contrast to the legionnaires he had seen the night before, who had a short sword and rectangle shield. The men lined up eight rows deep and ten wide. In front of each block there was a centurion. He recognised some of the faces through the helmets and cheek guards as the men he had met last night. All six centurions were there, with Tigris to the far right. Once all the men formed up, everyone stood in silence. Waiting.

Finally, a clip clop of hooves could be heard and a figure emerged from the grey darkness to Rafe's left. A small figure on a white stallion.

The figure pulled up next to Kate, and Rafe could make out the young face hidden behind the cheek guards of the ornate helmet crested with a large red plume.

"Prefect," the figure said.

Rafe recognised the voice of Octavian.

"Sir. We await your orders," Kate said as she stood to attention.

"No time like the present. Let's get going."

Kate gave the order, and the blocks of men stepped to their left. Then with a bark from the centurion's, the blocks moved off. Octavian kicked his heels into his white mare and raced to the head of the cohort where Tigris was, leaving Rafe with Kate.

"Come on then." Kate and Rafe walked at a brisk pace by the side of the column, making their way to the front. Kate whispered to Rafe, "My advice to you is to keep your head down. Keep safe, and let the men do the heavy lifting."

"Why? How bad is it going to get?" Rafe said

"Very bad," Kate said with a tinge of warning.

"Do you know what happens in this battle?" Rafe asked, his legs going to jelly.

"Yes," Kate said shortly.

"You do? So, what happens?" Rafe asked. He was relieved that at least he could be prepared for what was about to come.

"Julius and Octavian are right. The main attack is in the west, however the feint to the east where we are heading is a lot bigger than they anticipated."

His heart pounded. "You knew this. Why didn't you tell them?"

Kate pursed her lips and scowled. "History has already happened, and we are not here to change it, but to protect it."

They were near the front of the column now and could make out the top of Octavian's head who rode at the head on his horse. Rafe cast a look around to make sure no one was within earshot.

"So, Jupiter's son is Caeser then," Rafe whispering.

"As you have been informed," Kate replied bluntly.

"But he eventually gets stabbed in the back by his Senators, how does that further Jupiter's cause?" Rafe said

"You really don't know much about Roman history, do you?"

Rafe didn't answer, he was distracted by a rough looking dog, that ran in front of the column and was nearly trampled on by Octavian.

Kate continued without skipping a beat. "Julius Caesar conquers all of Gaul, which is modern day France. You may not know this but he was the first Roman General to step foot on the southern coast of England. However, where he really gains infamy is when he crosses the river Rubicon because when he does, he effectively takes control of the Empire and ends the Roman Republic. His adopted son." Nodding towards Octavian who was now only a few strides in front. "Becomes Rome's first Emperor, and one of its most successful. But you probably know him by the name of Emperor Augustus, which is the name he adopts later in life."

"Oh." The penny dropped "*The* Emperor Augustus will be that boy on the mount?"

"Yes. So, to answer your question, Jupiter's son, Caesar, helps pave the way for Rome to become one of the world's greatest Empires, and you ask how he furthered Jupiter's cause." She snorted with derision.

"Right, we're nearly there now so Octavian will call a cease to the marching. Remember what I said about letting your men take the brunt of it," Kate whispered.

Rafe started weighing up the arguments for fighting, to show leadership and courage, versus his survival odds by hanging back. "Kate, what happens if I were to get killed while fighting?" Rafe asked having never known the real answer to it.

"Then your friend Evie will be outliving you. If you get killed in here, you die like everyone else. You're still flesh and blood after all."

Sweat built up on his back. He wasn't sure if it was through his lack of fitness or what lay ahead.

In the sky, the dark shade of grey merged into a light grey, and Octavian shouted out an order to halt. The body of men stopping in a wave as the centurion's relayed the order down the line.

Kate marched to her superior, the bottom of her tunic from under the armour billowing behind her. After a brief exchange, which Rafe could not hear, Kate returned and cupped her hands. Rafe standing in awe at her relaxed demeanour.

"Right, you bunch of barbarians," hollered Kate.

The men responded with light-hearted chuckles.

"Let's get ready to spill some Gaulish blood."

The men roared, sending goosebumps across Rafe's body.

One by one, the blocks of soldiers were assigned their part of the palisade. Until only Octavian, Rafe and Kate were left.

Coming down the path, the trudging of feet and clanging of metal increased in volume.

"Prefects," Octavian said. "The other auxiliaries are here, take your stations."

Rafe followed Kate to the top of the spiked wall, where they climbed some steps.

"You will be with the sixth century," Kate informed Rafe. "They are positioned where the palisade is hardest to attack. Centurion Gallac leads there, he will defer to you because of your rank but listen to him, his experience is invaluable. Okay?"

"Will we get through this?" Rafe said with a broken voice.

"I hope so."

Rafe wanted to say he was scared but it would serve no purpose. His knees shook as he waded between the men, when he finally saw the crest of Centurion Gallac on a raised platform on the wall, and moved to stand beside him.

Through his cheek guards, Gallac had a flat nose and his chin jutted out. Their century was positioned facing inwards towards Vercingetorix's settlement which the Romans surrounded. Along the wall was an endless line of men, while behind on the wall facing outwards were more men watching for any reinforcements which might try and relieve Vercingetorix.

Rafe cast his mind home and his family but once he had exhausted that, his memory drifted off to the one place he rather avoid, which was school. For some reason, he dwelled on a situation at school when a boy in the lunch queue had poked him in the stomach so hard it actually hurt, and as he did so, the boy jeered telling him he was fat. All through lunch, he'd been paranoid in case that same boy came up to him, so had just pushed his food around on his plate. Rafe had gone to the bathroom afterwards and rubbed wet tissue under his arms to absorb some of his sweat.

Why he thought of that, he did not know. Perhaps the anxiety he felt brought up old memories.

Without even realising it, the light grey sky was now a muddy yellow, and the men started to murmur, as a line of horsemen approached. When did they appear, Rafe thought. A trumpet sounded close by, followed by other trumpets down the line which grew fainter the further down the line they got.

"Steady!" Barked out Centurion Gallac.

Other centurions could be heard calling out as well.

Where was Kate and Octavian? He searched around to locate them but had no luck. He needed to make sure Octavian stayed alive by the sounds of it

As the line of horsemen approached, kicking up dust, they screened the enemy body behind them. The sound of clashing steel and cries of men, echoed from somewhere afar.

Rafe glanced sideways at Centurion Gallac.

"The west, sir," Gallac mumbled. "The battle has commenced for the legionnaires then. Not to worry, it'll be our turn soon, and by the look of how large the enemy are, a bloody one it will be too."

Rafe couldn't help but give a tentative smile.

"Where's Octavian?"

"Further down the wall." Gallac nodded to the left.

Rafe finally spotted him in his sparkling armour and helmet with the longest red plumes sticking up. He was a sight to see. Octavian was positioned some way down the wall and surrounded by the biggest grouping of Roman soldiers, evidently there to protect him thank goodness.

"Not a subtle look, is it?" Rafe offered.

"He looks glorious, I think. Not many Generals or Tribunes take to the front lines, so he'll have the men's respect for it after."

In front, someone shouted, drawing everyone's attention.

With another shout, the horses at the front of the column parted and from behind the body of men, flowed forward with a roar reminiscent of a tidal wave. They dressed in all manner of mismatched armour and furs. Each holding their own weapon of choice; spears, long swords, stolen Roman short swords and different sizes of axes and hammers.

They stopped some distance from the defensive ditches but close enough that the snarls of the enemy in front could be seen. As the body of men swelled forward, Rafe could now see the back of the enemy units. It was a massive horde; wide, deep and moving like a wave. And most worryingly of all was the fact that it was far bigger than their own thin black line manning the wall. Kate was right, this was no feint, this was a two-pronged attack. One of the leaders on horseback circled around in the saddle of his horse and waved his sword in the air.

A shadow of lines arced into the sky.

"Shields!" Men shouted up and down the line. Rafe marvelled at the pinpricks of sticks hurtling towards him. Someone barged him in the side when raising their oval shield and suddenly, he remembered to do the same.

The clatter of arrows cracked around him, and the man next to him screamed and went down, clutching his foot where a wooden shaft of an arrow protruded out. Arms pulled him out of the way and another body filled his position. This was the efficiency of the Roman army first hand, he mused; next person up and everyone knowing their role, fulfilling it like a well-oiled machine.

Tentatively lowering his shield, he observed now had an arrow stuck in it. He tried prising it off and realised he was not strong enough and would sooner get a splinter than dislodge it.

"Fire!" Kate's voice bellowed from somewhere. Moving his head side to side to get a glimpse of where she was, he finally saw her standing between the palisades with a score of archers spaced out. They let loose, their arrows raising high overhead. The deadly arrows didn't hit the front ranks but rather the middle of the horde and the effect was instantaneous. With arrows raining down on them, the middle ranks pushed the front ranks and the tide of men surged forwards into a run.

The mass of bodies were only several paces when, it abruptly stopped with most of the front rank going to ground in a hail of screams.

What had just happened, Rafe wondered as howling and ear-piercing screams came from below. Only a handful of men lay motionless but the damage was done. The charge had been halted, and men with bloodied faces crawled along the floor or sat gripping their feet.

"What happened?" he said as a second volley of arrows hit the enemy, and the horde edged backwards.

"The Prefect." Gallac grinned widely behind his cheek guards. "She's a clever, that one. She got the blacksmith to make small caltrops, which are hard to see to a running man, especially in poor light."

Rafe must have been a picture of confusion as Gallac answered the very question that had been on his mind.

"Metal spikes you throw on the floor. They go right through your boots and are nasty things. I never liked them myself but they seem to have helped us today."

"So, what happens now?" Rafe said knowing he was beginning to sound like he didn't know what he was doing. Which of course he didn't.

"We wait. They will attack again."

The mounted leader rode along his battle lines, shouting words that lost in the clamour, but the meaning of which was clear. He rode up and down three times, with each lap more of the men took up banging their weapons against their shields.

A rider from across the battle line raced across the path of the front rank, skidding to a stop next to their leader. After a short deliberation, the new arrival, galloped away, circling the army and heading towards the rear of the host.

The enemy just stood banging and making a noise. Occasionally, someone would break from the line to hurl insults and challenges, but the Romans, to their credit, just stood and took it. Sporadic volleys of arrows would sail down on the lines in front, causing the enemy to raise their shields and fire a return volley.

Rafe started fidgeting with his tunic, clasping it in his hand, as the mass of men and their cajoling started to grate on him. He tugged at the armour, the sweat irritating the fold of his skin on his stomach. Where had that rider gone to?

He didn't have long to wait as the rider came slowly, and there was something behind it. Rafe tried to stand on his tip toes to get a better view.

As the enemy drew nearer slowly, wagons started to materialise in between the ranks of soldiers in front. Counting them as they appeared, Rafe could make out four of them, with two riders dragging each one.

With another roar from their leader, the host of men edged forwards slowly. When they reached the field of caltrops and the wailing injured on the floor, groups of men started pulling material from the wagons onto the ground in front of them. The shower of arrows from Evie's archers increased, falling towards the wagons. One of the riders slumped in his mount with an arrow protruding from his chest.

There were now four spikes of men moving ahead of the mass, and as they moved forward, they dropped material on the floor, covering the ground in thick piles. They were covering the hidden caltrops to open up paths to the palisade. One of the creeping spikes got ahead of the others, and was racing to reach the ditch in front of the palisade.

A shout from somewhere along the wall and the front rank of men on the Roman palisade rained down spears, causing several of the enemy and their loads to collapse to the floor. More men pressed forward to take up the material, dropping it forwards and to the sides, opening up their battle fronts.

As they snaked forwards, spears and arrows from the Romans rained down, leaving a trail of injured and dead men. The cries of the wounded causing Rafe to wince.

He never wanted to hear this sound again, it was excruciating.

When two prongs of the enemy reached the ditch, a mighty roar bellowed, and the damn of men surged forward over the bridge of material covering the caltrops. They ran down the ditch, then scrambled up to the other side and towards the palisade.

Even though Rafe wasn't in the front row, he was still petrified. A spear shot over his head to fall somewhere behind him.

The leader, still on his mount in the main mass of men on the other side of the caltrop field, placed something to his mouth. The horn blared a series of blasts, its hidden message lost on Rafe.

Behind, Rafe heard a louder horn, which made him jump. Why was there a horn coming from behind the Roman line? Craning his head back to get a better view, his heart lurched. There was another large force of men, behind them on the outer palisade. A detachment of the reinforcements sent to break the siege and free Vercingetorix.

He had no way of knowing how many of the enemy were in front of him on the inner palisade wall, but the outer palisade wall seemed to have as many. And certainly, many times over the Romans defending it.

We're all going to die, was the only thought on his mind.

What can I do to change the battle? I thought Evie said we would win, could she have been wrong? Would Caesar and Octavian be slain in this battle?

His attention was brought sharply back to focus when his helmet clanged. In the melee in front, a handful of men waved their arms in the air. What were they doing? In unison, they stopped waving and a flurry or rocks hit the palisade, but one hit the top edge of the wooden wall sending fragments scattering everywhere and one grazing his cheek. That stung.

"They're digging," someone shouted below the parapet.

"Sir." Centurion Gallac leaned towards him. "I would suggest you take three squads down below. If they dig deep enough, they can wrench our walls down and then we're all done for. We can hold them here. Go, sir!" A helmetless head in front of them poked up from the other side of the wall. Gallac leant forward and thrust his spear into it, sending it reeling back. "Squadrons two, four and five," Gallac shouted, "with the Prefect."

"With me!" Rafe bellowed as loud as he could, heading down the rampart. Wordlessly, and to his surprise, men followed. The ramp shuddered under their stamping feet.

Under the rampart, he found a handful of men, staring dumbly between the crack of the palisade planks. Rafe cast a quick glance, to see bodies scrabbling at the ground and worryingly one of the poles wobbled slightly.

"What do we do, sir?" One of the men asked.

What should we do? First, he needed to create a barricade.

"Form a shield wall in three ranks." Rafe remembered seeing soldiers in history books doing the same. "If anyone comes through you stab 'em with the pointy end."

A few men laughed.

"You three." He pointed to the closest men. "With me, we need to find something to fill in the breach." He ran a short distance from the palisade. Rafe spotted what he was looking for. Racing as fast as he could, he saw a wagon and started pushing.

"Heave, you lot," Rafe said.

The sound of heavy grunting was all around as the wagon rolled forwards with more momentum, Rafe let go and ran to the front to direct it. Arriving at the small shield wall in front of the palisade, one of his men thrust forward to stab into the face of a Gaul trying to crawl through the gap. One of the poles of the palisade had been dug up and the enemy were now working on another.

"Stand back," Rafe ordered.

The cart came at pace behind him, full of wooden stakes as long as the palisade. It crashed into the wall, shaking it. A man on the other side, who was working his hand around the second pole, cried out as his hand got trapped by the overladen cart.

"Use the poles to take the wheels off. Give me a hand." Grabbing a pole, Rafe nearly dropped it as he hadn't realised how heavy it was. Someone, to his relief, helped him. Jamming the pole in the arch of the wheel, they pushed and the wheel snapped off, collapsing on one side. Seeing what he had done, two men did the same to the other side. Now the cart would not shift, and it blocked a wide enough area of the wall but it was only waist high, low enough for the enemy to climb over.

"Grab a pole and wedge it between the gap and the palisade." In teams of two, the Romans began to heft the poles into their shoulders and place them on top of the cart along the wall. A horizontal criss-cross of poles took shape.

The enemy would have to dig up a dozen poles to get through now, Rafe mused, which if they tried would lose them a lot of men.

"Squadron two, stay here. Squads four and five, have we got any stone?"

"We have more timber," someone volunteered, whose breath was a little stale from last night.

"Stone would be preferable as we may need that timber for repairs."

"None spare that I know of," the soldier ventured.

"Damn!" While looking for something to use, he spied a giant of a man on the palisade swinging his axe wildly at the Roman defenders. The gap his swing created, opened up space for his comrades to form a foothold on the parapet. "Form up on me, two men a breast. Shields raised and spears forwards."

"What's the plan, sir?" a Roman shifting on his feet asked.

"We need to push that giant over the top. When we get there, we go as a unit as fast as we can and shields close together."

"We're ready, sir," one man on the side offered.

"That's why we're the best."

The man grinned a toothless smile and took his place.

"Quick march!" Rafe bellowed, heading towards the ramp up to the top. Rafe could feel his arm starting to throb, so he re-adjusted the grip on his weapon. What on earth was he thinking charging at a giant?

By the time he reached the short distance to the ramp that led to the raised platform, he wheezed and felt a stitch. The man next to him started to pull forward.

"Stay in line," Rafe managed to bite out through gasps. At the top, he took a deep gasp of air and would have stopped for a rest if it weren't for the men behind him.

Before him, he could now see how perilous their situation was. The Batavians were fighting one on one. While his auxiliaries had armour to give them protection, they were also heavy, and his forces would tire before the lightly armoured Gauls did, who were moving swiftly from one fight to another, darting in and out.

Rafe waved his men into a rough four-man line with four ranks. Rafe stood in the second rank. "Go in hard, pushing everyone over, even our own if need be. Back rank, you finish anyone off we walk over, except our own, of course."

"You want us to charge at our own, Prefect?" someone asked incredulously.

"Yes, but try not to fatally injure our own. We can't stop for anyone, you hear, we need to push the enemy back over the wall before it's too late. Now charge!" The group of two squadrons and Rafe sprinted in a line.

Rafe eyed an auxiliary that was on the floor with a Gaul, grappling with a knife between them. The front rank barrelled into them causing the Gaul to fall flat on the floor. Rafe jumped over, leaving the ranks behind to take care of the rest. Rafe knew his job was to add weight to the hammer of the front rank. As they encountered more one on one battles and pushed their way through the melee, their speed slowed to a walk.

"Shields interlock," he ordered as they now only crept forwards. Some of their own forces spied the safety of their wall and ran to join them, Rafe opened his shield to allow each one through.

Soon the chaos and melee developed into two lines. The Gauls taken aback by the Batavian counter attack, were now edging back with each step the auxiliaries advanced. A stream of Gauls started to cut their losses and climb back over the wall until only the giant was left, swinging his axe in an arc. Rafe half expected, perhaps a little naively, that he would realise his fate and scarper, instead the fearsome warrior charged forwards. His axe smashed into the man in front of Rafe, splitting the auxiliary troopers shield and crashing into his side. The force was so much the man crumpled to the ground in a heap. As the next person in line, Rafe stepped forwards, his knees shaking.

The warrior eyed Rafe, licking his lips. Rafe braced himself for impact when a javelin flew past his ear and narrowly missed the giant Gaul. Thinking himself lucky to still be alive, the giant of a man jumped over the palisade edge.

The men around Rafe thrust their spears in the air and cheered. Across the plain in front, where the host had been hammering on their walls, men now ran to safety and out of range of the archers that had been peppering them. Rafe wished the enemy would flee the battle entirely but they merely stood out of bowshot to regroup and lick their wounds.

Around them, Rafe spied Batavians and Gauls scattered on the floor, most were unmoving. He saw Gallac, with a nasty cut to his arm, laying on the floor and propped up on his elbows. Around him three Gauls lay in various unmoving positions.

"That was some fighting, Prefect," Gallac wheezed out breathlessly.

Rafe held his arm out, which Gallac grabbed and winced from the pain as he hauled himself up.

"I won't be ordered off the battlefield, sir," Gallac interjected.

"No, you won't. We need every good man and every good leader." He slapped the centurion on the shoulder.

Gallac dipped his head in thanks.

Holding his bloodied arm close to his chest, Gallac bellowed out. "Clear the ramparts and see to the wounded." At which men moved all about, busy at work.

Where was Kate? Casting an eye over to the other palisade, where men had held off an attack from the enemy relief force outside, he was relieved to see they were still holding them off. One Gaul had made it onto the parapet but was quickly dispatched by two auxiliaries.

He caught sight of a tall plume amongst the men on that palisade, spinning and thrusting. It was Kate.

He jogged down the ramp across the space between the two palisades and up the ramp on the other side to the wall which guarded the outside. Looking over the heads of the ranks of men, the enemy relief force was in larger numbers here. It seemed they were pinned back but causing the defenders issues,

"Kate!" Rafe yelled above the melee. "Kate!" His throat was sore and hoarse.

After dispatching a foe, Kate stepped back and heaved several big breaths.

"How... goes... it, Rafe?" Kate asked breathlessly.

"I'm having the time of my life! What do you think? How long can we keep this up for?" Rafe asked.

Kate answered with a smirk. "It won't last much longer now."

Before Rafe could answer, a trumpet echoed across the whole battlefield. A series of short blasts with different lengths. At that, a roar went up amongst the enemy outside of the gate, and the rear ranks started to run away. Not into the distance but along the wall.

"What's going on?" Rafe asked.

He wasn't the only one with the same idea, as the auxiliaries on this side started looking at each other and a few conversations broke out between them.

At that, a rider came galloping on a white mare down the middle of the thoroughfare between the outer and inner palisade.

"Prefect!" the rider called out.

Barging past, Kate ran down to meet the rider. Rafe pushed his way through also, panting as he tried to keep up. When he arrived, he heard only the last part.

"... the wall behind where Tribune Octavian is." The rider said.

Cupping her hands, Kate shouted so loud Rafe couldn't help but flinch.

"Auxiliaries stand to and form up. NOW!"

The next few moments sounded like thunder as the nailed boots thudded down the ramp to the thoroughfare between the walls. In a few moments, the soldiers formed up, some hunched nursing their injuries.

"Auxiliaries, we sprint to re-enforce the rear of Tribune Octavian. If they get past him, those barbarians will plough through here. Now let's go." Kate took off at a run.

Without another word, the unit followed her. They moved quickly with only the sound of armour clattering, and heavy breathing. Rafe kept up with Kate for a short period but after a few strides, she pulled ahead, and Rafe gave up trying to stay with her. His stomach muscles and legs aching.

Soldiers ran past him, and soon he was jogging slowly with what appeared to be the men who were nursing injuries. He hadn't done any exercise since he was last in the timeline, and he now regretted it. He had no idea of how far they had run but ahead, he saw the men fan across the mouth of the gap between the inner and outer palisade. Where was the red plume of Kate's helmet?

Joining the second rank of men, Rafe could see a small knot of men with Tribune Octavian in the middle surrounded by a flood of Gauls that came through a breach in the outer walls and swallowed up the small group of Romans.

The ferocity of the surging enemy was unlike anything Rafe had seen, as the enemy snarled, spat and swung their weapons.

Oh no! Rafe thought to himself, Octavian needed to live.

"March!" Someone ordered along the line.

A number of calls repeated along the line and almost as one, the front rank stepped forward, spears poking out the front. It wasn't long before they drew the attention of the enemy that was hammering at Octavian's red island of men.

"Push!" A deep voice commanded from nearby, and he saw a centurion plume to the right.

The soldier in front pushed forward, thrusting his spear as he went. As Rafe followed behind, he felt something under his feet. Peering down. his heart leapt to see a half-naked body. The man in front stumbled slightly and allowed a sword to poke through a gap in the shields, grazing the auxiliaries shoulder armour.

He felt a push from behind as men added their weight to their numbers. He felt crushed but their line edged forwards gradually. Again, Rafe stepped over another body, this time though it was thrashing around.

"Stab him, sir," a man next to him snarled, "before he cuts your tendons." The man grabbed a knife from his belt and thrust downwards to the sound of a gurgle. There was no time to ponder what had just happened, as the line kept moving forwards and the dead Gaul passed behind him.

Rafe moved a few more steps more, before the man in front stopped abruptly. A few shields to the right a man with an almighty large axe, swung at the shield wall. Two men either side of him poked their spears at an auxiliary, trying to tip the edge of the shield.

One unlucky Batavian succumbed to their tactics, as the spear tipped his shield, the axe swung down and lodged itself on the rim, ripping it from his grasp. Not able to let go in time, the Batavian stumbled forward, to be lost amongst the enemy that swelled towards the small opening. With knifes and swords flailing about, they hacked at the Batavian auxiliaries to enlarge the gap, allowing their comrades to join in the fight.

Rafe was no soldier but it didn't take an expert to know that if the Gauls created a wedge in their line, they would be able to attack from the front and sides, folding the thin line up on itself. Rafe pushed sideways towards the breach in their lines.

"Stab them!" He found himself calling. "Don't let them in!" He stabbed his spear over the head of a Batavian, causing a glancing blow to the chest of a Gaul with red paint on his face. "Close up!" Rafe ordered.

With renewed vigour, the Batavians stabbed forwards and pushed. Eventually closing the gap which threatened to open them up.

Rafe wanted to find out what was happening elsewhere, so pushed backwards. "Make way."

Once through, he spied almost two squadrons of archers with Kate forming into two lines. One group kneeling and the other standing.

"Rafe! Grab a dozen men to form up next to the archers."

"Why?" Rafe asked.

"Just get them!" She barked back.

Rafe searched for where he could grab some men from as he couldn't take any off the thin line holding the enemy back. Luckily, he spotted an Optio leading a group who were just joining the back ranks.

Rafe jogged as best he could to the junior officer. "Optio, bring your men with me."

"Yes, sir." The Optio waved his small group to follow Rafe and they formed up as per Kate's instructions.

"When I give the order, charge," Kate commanded.

Rafe wasn't sure what she was playing at until he saw how the middle part of the line holding the enemy back was buckling under the pressure of the Gauls throwing themselves at the Batavian shield wall. The Gauls were almost bursting through!

"Archers, ready," Kate ordered, and a chorus of bow strings being pulled emanated all around. "Steady. Steady."

As the black line of Batavian soldiers split open, Kate called the order and the first set of arrows hit half a dozen Gauls. Another set of arrows followed straight after, hitting the Gauls who stood behind. Kate called for both ranks to fire another round each, stemming the flow of Gauls breaking through.

"Everyone, charge!" Kate shouted, drawing her weapon and pointing it forwards.

The Optio and his contingent of men dressed in black, ran forwards. Knowing he was bulky but weak, Rafe stayed towards the back of the group.

To the credit of the Optio, he hit the Gauls before they knew what was happening. Already whittled down from the arrows, the Gauls fell to the floor, barged by the heavy shields of the auxiliary unit. The front rank, ploughed onwards, leaving their fallen foe to be finished off by the Batavians at the back.

With the small group of re-enforcements, the black line was once again secured and it once started pushing the enemy back inch by inch.

Rafe bent over with his hands on his knees, sucking in deep breaths, feeling exhausted. Eventually he gained enough composure to stagger over to Kate.

"That was a clever move," Rafe said breathlessly.

"I knew where they would be a breach the shield wall. Doing what we did, saved a lot of lives."

"A bit like the caltrops in front of the palisade," Rafe offered with sly smile.

"Come on, if history is going to plan, then Octavian is about to be saved."

Pushing their way forward to the front rank, Rafe felt the easing of tension in the fight. The enemy were retreating step by step but the clash of fighting still echoed across the battle. Then, without warning, the back ranks of the enemy dissipated. Chaos engulfed them, which was now mixed with the red tunics and metal helmets of the Roman legionnaires who had joined the fight from the other side.

"Forward!" Kate barked and stepped forwards. The black line of Batavian auxiliaries moved as one, their deadly spears aimed towards the enemy.

Seeing there was little hope between the advancing killing machines of the red legionnaires and black auxiliaries, the front line of Gauls also broke.

The rest of the battle was a blur, as the enemy were routed and hacked at from behind until there was no surviving Gaul in between the outer and inner palisades.

With the breach now stemmed and the battle won, Rafe placed his arms above his head trying to catch his breath. A lot of the men were now facing towards a knot of impressive looking soldiers. Octavian! His arm was held aloft by no other than Julius Caesar. Caesar's expression was stern, as though victory was always certain, the fabric on his arm was torn and a red line dripped through it.

Rafe breathed a sigh of relief. Thank goodness they were both alive.

"Caesar! Caesar! Caesar!" A chant started growing in noise as more men took it on, fists pumping the air. The euphoria was infectious, Rafe could feel the elation uplifting his tired body. His arms ached, his legs ached and he wanted to be sick but he didn't care. They had won! He had survived a Roman battle, seeing at first hand the efficiency of the Roman army, which would systematically roll over the Mediterranean states and beyond.

Leaning over, he couldn't stop himself as his stomach wretched and phlegm spat out. Wiping spittle on the back of his hand, he held his hands on his knees.

The men were still chanting and someone barged into him, almost sending him sprawling,

A round object with its lid off was held in front of his eyes. He took the flask and gulped at it until the acrid burning in his throat was gone.

"Thanks." He handed it back to Centurion Gallac who was stood next to him.

"Good work, sir." Gallac nodded his thanks, before pushing his way to join the celebrations.

Rafe could feel his lungs burning from all the running, pushing and... fighting. He didn't dare think about the atrocities he had committed; he would dwell on it another time. He was so tired, he hadn't done any exercising since Greece. And with the thought of Greece came Cleon, or whatever his name was, and Evie laying in a bed hooked up to machines that beeped intermittently.

Eyeing the crowds around him, he wondered what there was to celebrate as nothing had changed. Rafe moved away from where the mass of men was, barging soldiers out of the way, or at least trying to, as many of them were stronger than him. At the back of the crowd of soldiers, two men in front pulled at some Gaulish knife they had found.

"Move!" Rafe growled, pushing past them. He needed air, so he made his way to a ramp where a few soldiers manned a parapet. Walking up it with his now stiff legs, he stared out over the outer wall once he reached it. The enemy were in the distance and getting smaller. Squadrons of Roman horse mowed down any stragglers. Hopefully, that was the end of fighting, Rafe mused, he didn't know if he could take another day of it. He was sore all over and he rubbed the loose skin around his neck. He couldn't go on like this, being unable to move so much, aching and breathless at any inkling of exercise, plus, he had to admit he liked how Centurion Gallac had looked at him. Rafe promised he would go for a run tomorrow, but suspected it would be another promise broken.

Evie, how can I bring her back, he mused. He rested his arms flat against the wooden stakes which made the wall.

He stood like that for a few minutes when someone asked him, "Penny for your thoughts?"

He hadn't noticed her arrive but it was Kate.

"Evie. I was just wondering how I could bring her back," Rafe replied solemnly.

Kate was silent for a minute before she answered. "I'll be honest, I haven't heard of anything which can bring people back from the brink of death. When a Grey Guardian is injured, we take them back to The Fates and they look after them and heal them."

"Will I meet them? The other Grey Guardians?" Rafe wondered aloud.

"Maybe one day. They are a great bunch." A rare chuckle escaped Kate's lips, he didn't think she could laugh.

"Sisi, she's quick as anything. She has short, dark hair, brown eyes and she grew up in Japan where she learnt martial arts so she fights like a ninja. She never stops eating and is always quick with words." Kate brushed a loose piece of hair out of her face. "Anika, she doesn't fight much but she knows absolutely everything and literally never stops reading. You can't miss her as she always has a long plait with her thick brown hair. Then there's Dax, who is a nutcase and solid as anything. No idea where he is from though, as we can never get it out of him. You have to be careful of him though, as he's loyal as anything but it's always about the mission with him. No matter what the cost is."

Again, that weird silence with her.

"Just the four of you then, that's not many."

A sad thoughtful grimace scrunched up Kate's face. "There used to be more of us," she continued, "but some left."

"Left?" The idea that there was even an option had never occurred to him.

"Sure, if you have a good enough reason, you can leave anytime you want. Guardians leave for all sorts of reasons. Can't cut it or want to start a family, are some of the most popular reasons. When I first joined, a girl called Lucy took me under her wing, and I cried for a month when she left as she wanted to go to college, get a job and have her own kids. I don't see the appeal to be honest." Kate scrunched up her face, making her freckles stand out.

"Really? Why not?" Rafe asked.

"Maybe once I would have considered having a family, but not now." She gave a heavy sigh. "Other than some Grey Guardians choosing to leave, on rare occasions one dies or goes missing. Not often but it happens."

"When was the last one?" Rafe asked before realising his mistake as he spoke, these were her friends and his curiosity would seem callous to her.

"A year ago," Kate answered slowly.

Rafe wanted to ask more but horns were blown which stopped any more conversation. Searching the outer wall, there were no enemy warbands approaching, in fact, only dribs and drabs of horsemen trotted back from their pursuit.

"Inner wall," Kate said

In the distance, a party of men approached.

"Who's that?" Rafe asked, rubbing his arms from where they had been leaning on the palisade.

"Vercingetorix, he's going to surrender."

Chapter Eight

Rafe stood in the great tent which had been erected for the victory celebrations. Inside was full officers of every rank. On the top table, Julius Caesar was flanked by Mark Antony and Senior Tribune Octavian. They toasted each other, clashing their mugs together and sloshing liquid on the table.

Rafe milled through the crowd, watching the Roman officers talking and laughing. The regular soldiers were not invited to this celebration, they were having their own outside, and probably more raucous.

Centurion Gallac stumbled into Rafe and passed a drink to him. Rafe could make out little of what Gallac said to him, before he stumbled back through the crowd.

Rafe took a sniff at the contents and wrinkled his nose. Spying a table close by, he placed the cup down as he passed.

He didn't have time to join in on any of the talk or singing, his eyes were firmly on the top table. He watched, taking notes of each person's demeanour. It was obvious that Mark Antony was the opposite of Julius Caesar. Mark was toasting every man that passed their table, and laughing whenever he could. Slim, dark haired and confident he would clearly command the attention of any room he walked into. To be Julius Caesar's confident and right-hand man, he was undoubtedly a good General.

Caesar on the other hand, was a picture of contrast as he sat quietly, his eyes darting left and right, taking everything in. He had the look of a master tactician. His arm, which had been injured in battle, undoubtedly had a bandage hidden under his clothes.

Then next to him, sat Octavian, the young Senior Tribune, destined to be the first Emperor of Rome one day. He was the mirror image of Caesar, watching his surroundings and occasionally leaning in to Caesar saying something.

Watching the three intently, Rafe knew he needed to make sure Cleon didn't drop in on them and hurt Caesar or Octavian.

Next to Rafe, a group of officers cheered, distracting him. Rafe peered to see two men close together, arm wrestling. One of them was a centurion from the Batavian Cohort, the name Hurix came to mind from the other night.

The men shouted their support for their preferred competitor as a new round started. Most of the men who were watching wore the red tunics of the legionnaires, these cheered loudest for the man opposite Hurix.

Rafe whispered, "Come on, Hurix."

Hurix gritted his teeth, the veins in his arm bulging.

Rafe risked it a little louder this time. "Go on, Hurix!" An Optio spun to see who the new supporter was, he eyed Rafe up and down, clocking Rafe's Batavian garments.

Now with more force so that all the supporters heard, Rafe shouted, "GO ON, HURIX!"

Slowly Hurix forced his opponent's hand down to groans from the crowd. As it slammed on the table, the Roman opposite hung his head, while Hurix stood arms in the air cheering himself, noticing no one else cheered. Rafe punched his fist high and roared, "Batavian Cohort."

Hurix saw his superior and grasping Rafe's fist that was raised in the air, he grinned. "Batavia!" Hurix roared before releasing Rafe's hand, and making his way to the bar where some of the Batavian offers stood. They greeted with Hurix with back slaps.

That sort of camaraderie and friendship gave Rafe butterflies, and it was times like this he missed talking to Evie. She'd no doubt have something intellectual to say about the whole situation. He didn't want to think about it too much, as the image of her in a hospital bed came to mind again. If roles were reversed, she would know what to do, how to cure him. There must be a way, he reminded himself.

Watching the chaos unfold around him was much like school, people descending into animals. Thankfully as a Prefect, at least his rank prevented him from being pushed around here, no one chanted *big big Rafe* or taunted him for his weight.

Rafe gave a heavy sigh and cast a look for Kate, whom he couldn't see anywhere.

Casting a look at the top table and feeling torn between his mission and finding Kate. He decided a few minutes away wouldn't hurt, so walked outside to see if she was out there. Outside the tent flaps, there were six sentries standing guard, then further ahead another ring of more legionaries. Security was tight for this party.

In the torchlight and beyond the two lines of guards, campfires dotted the tent lines casting the shadows of men onto the sides of tents. There was much cheering and laughter from all around them.

One shadow though, caught his attention.

The shadow passed a fire, where some soldiers had a spit with a large animal and were currently turning it over. As some of the animal fat hit the fire, large flames sizzled higher and the shadow brightened to reveal a pale face and long wavy brown hair tied up.

Kate?

Rafe marched through the two rows of sentries, who each gave a cursory glance as he passed through. He nodded to the last sentry, to ensure he was recognised when he returned, although his black uniform would stand him out.

He brought his attention back to the tent lines and to where he thought he'd seen Kate. There! Her face, half cast in the light of a fire, weaved between the tents.

Rafe broke into a jog. Closing in, he stumbled over a rope holding a tent up.

"Argh!" Rafe yelled.

"Oi!" A figure from inside cursed him.

Dusting himself down, he cast his eye around but there was no sign of Kate.

Picking the direction which he thought she had gone, he began to run, his sword clanking against his leg. Chafing as it rubbed up and down.

"Kate?" Rafe whispered in between the tent lines. "Kate?"

To his right, two or three tents away, a figure darted by. Rafe swerved around a campfire, which a dozen men were singing around, and he headed towards the direction the figure had run. As he skipped around another tent rope, he realised he had inadvertently gone back on himself and was heading back towards Caesar's tent.

He felt bile rise up as he tried to sprint. His muscles still ached from the morning's battle.

Ahead, he saw the figure, standing still at a cross section of tents.

When Rafe reached the crossroads, he placed his hands on his knees and panted heavily. "Ka...te." Rasping between breaths.

Kate whipped her head around. "Rafe, what are you doing here?"

"Ye...s" He continued to gasp through breaths. *Oh* his lungs hurt.

Kate frowned at him.

He'd seen that look a million times before and knew what it meant. The pitying look of someone that wants to say how I need to do more exercise or eat less, but not wishing to say the obvious and cause an awkward moment.

"What are you doing here?" She asked again.

"I came... out for some air and to look for you... they are like animals in there." He said breathing heavily.

"Have you been out here long or have you only just come outside?" Kate asked tentatively.

"I've just come outside."

"Are you sure? Like, how long ago?" Her voice was rising.

"Just now," Rafe said a little unsure of what was into Kate.

"How long ago?" She was almost shouting it now and Rafe took a step back. Kate was scaring him, like the other night.

"About one minute ago. I came out of the tent and saw you across the way, passing those men roasting something on a spit."

Rafe thought that would relax her but she became more erratic, looking side to side. Her long wavy hair in a pony tail swished one way then another, brushing against his face.

"What's the matter?" Rafe said, he wanted to reach out a hand to comfort her but he dared not, given the mood she was in.

She moved her head in a semi-circle in search of something. Then suddenly, she swivelled on the spot to look behind them.

"Kate, what's going on?" Rafe was so scared he was on the verge of losing it. Thankfully though, her head snapped in his direction. Her face had a confused look about it.

"Um. I thought I saw someone," Kate stuttered.

"Who?" Rafe asked.

"Someone I know. Someone that shouldn't be here."

"Who?" Rafe pressed more forcefully.

Kate chewed her lip, not answering.

"You seem worried, and I'm a little scared if I'm honest," Rafe said.

"I'm worried too." Kate was again searching around them, spinning around on the spot, ignoring Rafe.

If she's worried, then I need to be worried too, Rafe thought. "Do we need to get back to watching Caesar?" He was conscious of why they were actually here.

He couldn't see her face in the shadowed light, but the intake of breath said it all. Without a word, she bolted. Rafe ignored the ache of his stomach muscles and chased after her.

They weaved and stumbled through the tent lines. Breathlessly drawing up to the line of sentries outside the officer's tent.

Kate was there first speaking to someone that had challenged her. "...we are Prefects of the Batavian auxiliaries."

The guards lumbered casually to the side, as though there was no urgency. Rafe noted a small sneer on one of the guards faces as they passed by. The next set of guards did not challenge them as they passed through.

Passing the tent flaps, the noise and smoke hit Rafe like a wall and he couldn't help but cough.

"I don't remember it this smoky before," Rafe managed between rasping breaths.

"Let's get to somewhere where there's ventilation. This smoke isn't good for us," Kate suggested.

Following her back through the haze towards the back, she found a table with no occupants and took a seat. Her arms were on the table, eyes darting about.

"So, what now?" Rafe asked, eyeing the tables closest to them, to see what Kate was looking for.

"We wait and we watch," Kate said sternly.

"Since we're going to be here a while," Rafe suggested, "Let's talk."

"Fine. What do you want to talk about?" Kate said, again she made no eye contact.

"Oh, I don't know, how about the fact you're being strange. Who are you looking for?" Rafe ground his teeth. This was getting frustrating.

"I thought I saw someone," Kate said still not looking at Rafe.

"Who?" Rafe flopped his arms onto the table with a bang. He was exasperated by asking the same question.

"I'll tell you if I see them," Kate said, chewing her lip again.

Rafe could tell he wasn't going to get anywhere by constantly asking, so something else popped in his head. He rubbed his chin as he worked the words into his mouth. "It seems like the Grey Guardians are... what's the word, not very well thought of."

"It's been like that for a while, from what I understand," Kate offered. "There used to be a lot of us from what I read once in The Fates' library. They weren't paying attention so I had a peek and flicked through a few pages in one of their books. From what I could tell, the Grey Guardians were not only many in number but were well respected by the whole of HOG and the shadow world."

"What happened?" Rafe asked, surprised by this.

"Beats me. But let's be honest, we're a handful of kids, who are slightly pathetic. Would you place respect in that?" Kate finally made eye contact at this. A loose strand of her wavy hair fell down her face,

"There must have been a reason why they lost that respect," Rafe said.

"Well, if there is a reason, no one has said anything about it to me." Kate flicked the loose strand behind her ear, and went back to watching the crowd.

Rafe picked at a knot in the wooden table casually. "Where was that book?"

"First book on the second shelf, you're not thinking of stealing it, are you?" Kate said.

"Maybe. I don't know yet, I know someone who'd like to read it one day." And when I figure out a way to bring her back, perhaps she can give us some answers, Rafe thought.

"Why are you so bothered anyway?" Kate's wavy hair tied in a pony tail flicked back and forwards as her head kept moving.

"I'm curious," Rafe answered. Without warning, someone bumped into him from the side, nearly toppling him off his stool.

"Something is happening." She nodded over to a knot of people stood up in a group, the tent's noise grew deadly quiet. A man moved out of Rafe's way, opening up a brief view of Caesar, Antony, Octavian and a few men who stood facing the crowd.

"Officers of the Fifth Alaudae," someone called out.

A cheer went up from a handful of men sat down.

"The Eighth Augusta." Rafe saw through a gap that it was Caesar who was naming the armies legions.

And a different group cheered, louder than the last. Each time Caesar announced the Legion's name a cheer went up. "The Ninth Hispania, the Tenth Fretensis, the Eleventh Claudia, the Twelfth Fulminata, the Thirteenth Gemina and Fourteenth Gemina." He paused after each cheer. Then someone banged a table, which was followed by another bang. Rafe twisted around to see Centurion Tigris and the rest of the officers of the

Batavian auxiliaries at a table. Next to them on another table, were the two Prefects from the Remi Cohort, and their officers.

Both tables banged their fists on the tables.

All the Roman soldiers around watched, as the auxiliaries' banged their fists louder and faster. Kate joined in, and a few Roman soldiers close by in their red tunics, stepped back from them. Rafe felt himself swept up in the moment, and joined in.

While most of the Romans stood silently or with mouths wide open, more and more tables and groups of standing men banged whatever was to hand. A jug, a cup, their hands, their feet or a slap to the knee.

"And the brave..." Caesar shouted above the hammering noise. "The defiant... the stalwart soldiers, of the Batavian and Remi Cohorts." A big cheer went up from around the tent. But not from all, Rafe noted, some stood still, frowning their disapproval. "Without whom the Eastern wall would have been overrun."

"And lastly, to the soldier that stopped a spear thrust, that would have found its mark." Caesar took a step to the side and a young man stepped forward. Even in the dim light, Rafe could still make out the familiar sandy hair, nose and beaming smile.

He was sure his heart stopped beating for a few moments, for he had to gasp to take a breath. It couldn't be, could it?

Kate next to him was equally stunned into silence with her mouth agape. Although Rafe didn't think anything could shock her, one thing was clear, Kate recognised that sandy haired person as much as he did.

Caesar was speaking again but his words were lost on him.

Mouth dry, Rafe licked his lips. "Do you..." he croaked. He cleared his throat. "Do you know him?"

Kate wide eyed, stared right through Rafe.

"Kate! I said, do you know him?" Rafe shouted now and banged his fist on the table.

Her hands began to shake.

"Kate! I need to know" Rafe hissed. "Do you recognise that person?"

"Yes." A tear fell down her cheek. "Yes, I do. It's Sebastian. He was a Grey Guardian once."

Oh no! Rafe thought. That wasn't Sebastian to him, that was Cleon, his friend he met in Ancient Greece and was a mercenary from Macedonia. Someone who should not be in this timeline but a few hundred years earlier in history. So, Cleon and Sebastian were the same person, and more worryingly, he was a Grey Guardian once. Which, whatever way you put it, was bad news.

Sebastian's arm was still being held aloft by Caesar, and he beamed to the crowd gathered around.

Words from the front started to pierce the fog that had clouded Rafe's head. ".... with men like this... Invincible.... no one..." The rest was lost but everyone raised their jugs and chanted.

"Hail Caesar. Hail Caesar. Hail Caesar." The room chorused.

Everyone except him and Kate, which did not go unnoticed.

Sebastian stared at them with his head cocked to the side. The smile he held not faltering.

He felt the table shift as Kate stood up. Rafe made to grab her top and felt her strain against him. "Don't," Rafe pleaded.

"Let go," Kate hissed.

"If you storm up there and attack the man who saved Caesar's life, what do you think all these men will do to you?" Rafe said.

The pressure tugging at his hand waned and once she stopped struggling, Rafe let go. Kate made her way slowly around one side of the table, so Rafe made to follow but a group of men stumbled into his path. Kate was now a handful of paces ahead and was picking up pace, so Rafe side stepped and made his way around the group. One tugged at his arm and cheered, eyes glazed. Rafe yanked his sleeve away and pushed his way through, knocking a drink out of someone's hand.

"Oi, auxiliary!" It was a Roman centurion. shaking his wet hand where the drink had spilt. The other hand grabbed Rafe by his shirt.

"I'm sorry," Rafe stuttered.

"That's not good enough. You've spilt my drink and now my arm is wet, you'll pay for that." The Roman snarled with droplets of spit hitting Rafe.

"I wouldn't do that if I were you," someone said next to them.

Rafe was relieved to see the bald-headed face of Centurion Tigris. "That's a Prefect, centurion, and therefore, your superior."

The Roman centurion growled and let go, then disappeared into the crowd.

"Thanks," Rafe said, wishing he could have thanked him more but he pushed his way even harder between men. He needed to find Kate.

He saw the flick of Kate's hair in the smoke-filled crowd, heading towards the exit. He made a beeline for it.

When he was out, he stood in front of a sentry guard.

"Where did the Prefect go?" Rafe shouted causing the sentry take a step back. "Where?"

Finally, he pointed his spear. "That way."

Rafe ran as fast as he could weaving in between tents. To his relief he saw the silhouette of Kate on the floor in front of Sebastian. It was dark in this area of tents, the only light coming from a campfire some distance away.

Rafe hobbled the last few strides, his legs were sore from all the fighting that morning.

In the dim light he could see sparkles down both Kate's cheeks. As she kneeled on the floor, Sebastian crouched down, caressing her cheek affectionately with one hand and holding her hand with the other.

They were whispering to each other. "I... sorry... the only way..."

When Rafe drew up taking in deep breaths, Sebastian stood.

"Hello Rafe," the familiar face said.

Rafe wondered what to say to someone who you know has betrayed you and nearly killed your friend.

"I've missed you, Rafe." Sebastian held his hand out but Rafe just stared at it and clenched his fists.

"You nearly killed Evie," Rafe finally roared out.

Sebastian dropped his hand. Was that a frown that darkened his face? "That was an accident."

"Why did you do it?" Rafe pleaded loudly.

"I wasn't aiming for her," Sebastian said nonchalantly, avoiding answering the question.

"Who then?"

"It doesn't matter. Rafe, you were my friend, I would never hurt you. I see a lot of myself in you, you see."

The weight of the bracelet he had been given by Cleon, felt heavier than usual. "So should I call you Cleon, or Sebastian then?"

At that, the traitor in front of him cast a gaze down at Kate and stroked the top of her head gently. She was still sobbing.

"A necessary disguise unfortunately but you are correct, my name is Sebastian."

Rafe couldn't help but just shake his head. Everything Sebastian said, just boiled his blood, he felt ready to explode. Unknowingly, his hand went to the pommel of his sword.

"Evie is in hospital, hooked up to monitors to keep her alive. You need to come with me to help heal her."

"I can't do that?" His voice was like silk.

"Why not?"

"There's something I need to do first. If you come with me, I can show you how the world can be a better place. The world is corrupt, and it needs to change. I can fix it. Once I have done that, I can come with you to help Evie. Come, I can take both of you." He took a step back to lead the way.

Kate raised her head.

Rafe wondered if she meant to go with him?

Rafe, surprising himself, drew his sword. The rasp of metal stopped Sebastian in his tracks.

"You know I'm a better fighter than you. You would lose."

"You have to help Evie." Rafe felt the sweat in his hand as he gripped the sword.

"I can't, there is something greater and more important I have to do. More important than you and I."

"I can't let you go." Rafe's arm shook, and his knees were numb.

"Ah, I am sorry, Rafe," Sebastian said pityingly. "I have to go now. Kate, are you coming?"

Kate's head was still raised and cast in shadow so Rafe make out her facial expression.

"Kate, you can't." Rafe stepped forward.

Sebastian suddenly spun and kicked Rafe in the chest. It happened so fast that Rafe stumbled backwards, the breath knocked out of him. Even though he was shocked that Sebastian had hit him, he also knew he could have hurt Rafe a lot more if he had wanted.

"Come, Kate?" Sebastian called louder and extended his hand. Kate had raised onto one knee now.

"No, Kate... you can't." Rafe managed through clenched teeth. What was wrong with her! Why was she just kneeling on the floor?

"Fine, Kate, have it your way." Sebastian made to leave, and Rafe lunged to grab him. "You can't go," Rafe begged but Sebastian only shook him off, sending him to the ground.

Sebastian moved his arms forwards and a line appeared, then without another word, he stepped through and closed it up behind him.

Rafe knew then that they were in a world of trouble.

From behind him, he could hear the sobs and sniffling of Kate, but he was so angry he didn't care for them. Kate needed to give him answers.

Chapter Nine

Rafe paced inside of the tent, hand clasped in front as though praying when, in reality, he was squeezing his hands hard together. The tension passed through his body and out through his hands.

The anger in him wanted to just kick something. The fear and worry wanted him to puke. The shame in him wanted to run from this tent and back to his life. He couldn't care less if he didn't see Kate and Sebastian again, who was Cleon until a few minutes ago. But he also knew that the only way he was going to find a way to bring Evie back, was by being part of this world.

"I'm sorry I didn't help you stop Sebastian." Kate sniffled.

Rafe looked down at her. Her hair had gone matted and draped over her face as she leant forwards staring at the floor. She hadn't made eye contact with him since that meeting with Sebastian, not even while he half dragged her back to the tent. They'd got some funny looks along the way, and Rafe had half a thought to feign drunkenness but the mixture of emotions in him wouldn't allow that. Especially the anger.

"What were you doing with him when he was stood there?" Blasted Rafe, hoping no one outside of the tent would hear.

The lack of answers wasn't helping him contain the growling beast inside.

"Kate!" Rafe shouted.

For the first time, she whipped her face around, her eyes were glazed and struggled to focus.

"Tell me everything," Rafe demanded. "He was here for a reason, and it's important I know everything. He was here where the son of Jupiter is and previously in Ancient Greece with the son of Zeus. We are in big trouble unless you tell me everything."

"Water please," Kate whispered meekly.

"What?" Rafe knew he was a little terse with her but he wanted answers now.

"Water please," Kate croaked a little louder.

Rafe was so angry with Kate, for nearly leaving with Sebastian and from hiding something from Rafe. He searched about the small tent and found a jug by a washing bowl, he swirled the contents to see how much was left and handed it to her. He couldn't be bothered to find a cup to fill it with, for all he cared, she could drink from the jug and spill it down her clothes.

Which Kate did as she gulped it down. She smacked her lips after she finished. Rafe couldn't help but watch her every movement, waiting for a sign.

"Your bracelet." Kate nodded towards Rafe.

Rafe rubbed his wrist, feeling the familiar feeling of the gift under his sleeve.

"It's a Grey Guardian's bracelet," Kate said.

"I know," Rafe said tersely.

"When I saw it on you. A part of me knew it was his but I didn't want to believe it, how could it be his when he was dead? Sebastian found it a long time ago. It's a relic from the Grey Guardians of past, he treasured and always wore it. Until he gave it to you it seems."

"Who is Sebastian, really?" Rafe questioned.

"He was a Grey Guardian, the best of us, and he was... my boyfriend until he went missing without a trace, we all thought he'd been killed." Kate's bottom lip wobbled.

"What?" Rafe sidled up to Kate, realising why she had been hit so hard by his appearance.

"Sebastian was our leader, he took care of The Grey Guardians, and he was also very good at protecting the timeline. Most of the shadow world will know of him, he was fearless and always respectful to the shadow creatures. Always. Then one day, he was on a mission, and he never came back. No one ever heard from him again. We searched and searched but there was no trace of him, the days became months, then they became years, then finally, The Fates declared, they would stop looking. I cried for a week after that, Anika thought I'd gone insane because I was so hysterical. So, when I saw that bracelet on your wrist, I didn't want to believe it. But then I saw him in the tent standing next to Julius Caesar. Why didn't he let anyone know he was alive? Why didn't he contact me? We loved each other." Kate trailed off.

"So, your boyfriend is back from the dead. But at the end of the day, he's part of the enemy now," Rafe wondered out aloud. "So, what did he say to you?"

"I don't..."

"He must have said something to you? We need to know, as the fate of the world is at stake here Kate." Rafe pushed.

"I begged him to tell me what was going on. The only thing he said of note was that *things were about to change for the better.*"

Rafe stood and tried to piece it all together; what did it all mean and why did he leave so suddenly from this timeline? Caesar and Octavian were both still alive but his mission must have been completed. Then again, thinking about Greece, The Fates said that Sebastian left just after he, Evie and Heracles entered the gateway to the Underworld, although Zeus did vanish not long afterwards. Sebastian wasn't trying to kill the sons and daughters of god and alter time, Rafe decided, he was doing something else.

"He likes you, you know." Kate's voice was soft in the dim light of the tent.

That stopped Rafe in his tracks "Huh?"

"Yes, he had a sort of look in eye. Once I saw it, I knew he would also offer to take you with him. He always drew people into him."

Rafe couldn't shy away from how Kate used the word *also,* for he had forgotten that Kate could have left with him. But she had decided to stay, like Rafe.

"I'd never have gone with him," Rafe clarified.

The strong-willed girl he thought nothing could break, now seemed pitiful before him. Would she have decided to go if Rafe hadn't come? Rafe watched her as she sat and said nothing.

"He hurt Evie, and she may never recover because of him. You need to realise he isn't the person you once loved," Rafe said.

"There must be some explanation."

Rafe couldn't believe what he was hearing. "What are you talking about? He's stolen part of the Book of Sorothir from Angelic Order Arndell, he made Zeus disappear, and he left a trail of bodies behind him in Greece."

Rafe was feeling a little frustrated and rubbed his head until he could feel it burn.

"He wouldn't have done it without reason, that's not what he's like," Kate said a little livelier.

Was she blind, Rafe thought. Then something snapped inside him. "HE ALMOST KILLED EVIE!" Rafe yelled, making his throat hoarse. He knew she wasn't dead but she felt as good as. "He threw a knife knowing there was a risk it would hit us, yet he still threw it anyway. He's a murderer and he faked his own death."

Rafe paused to take in some breaths to slow the freight train his anger was riding. "What's worrying me is that you seem to still be in love with him." Rafe noticed how out of everything he'd said, it was this last part that made Kate's shoulders sag even more. The truth of it shattering any last dregs of resolve she had.

"It's not like I can switch off my feelings for him," Kate murmured. "I was and still am... in love with him."

Rafe saw a tear drop to her lap, creating a dark patch on her clothes.

Rafe stepped gently towards her. "Would you have gone with him if I weren't there?"

"I...I... don't know," Kate admitted.

That was worrying, Rafe thought.

"Whatever he came here for, he's got it. Do you know what it was?" Rafe said, still speaking in a low voice.

Kate shook her head.

"We need to tell The Fates about this now."

"What will you tell them?" Kate lifted her face which was streaked with rivers of tears.

"I don't know, to be honest." Rafe sighed. "Let's find Sherlock and see if he's still here, we need to tell someone what's going on."

They ambled through the tent lines. Rafe patted the familiar shape of Prometheus' blood in his pocket, which he was paranoid of losing.

It wasn't long before they found Sherlock and his market stall, having meandered there in a daze. This time, he was stationed near a Roman legion, rather than the side of the palisade close to the auxiliaries. Rafe eyed a bowl of watery meat someone had purchased from him and wrinkled his nose.

"Sherlock," Rafe called out.

"Ah Rafe and Ka...." He trailed off seeing the tear-stained streaks down her face.

Rafe knew what was on his lips but he didn't have the will power to explain the whole story. "We need to see The Fates. The enemy have been and gone from this timeline."

"Shush." Sherlock waved his hands to keep his voice down. A group to the side cast furtive glances in their direction. "What?" Sherlock said in a hushed tone.

"We saw him. He's a..." Rafe stopped himself. He didn't know if he should unmask Sebastian before telling The Fates. What if people stopped trusting the Grey Guardians because of Sebastian.

"What's wrong with Kate?" Sherlock said.

"That's part of why we need to see The Fates now. Please can you get them a message?"

Sherlock stood still looking between the two of them.

"Sherlock, please." Rafe pleaded.

"I'll go now. Watch my stall and make sure no one helps themselves." He disappeared into the tent flap behind his stall.

Kate stood next to him just staring and not saying a word. If it were Evie, he would put his arm around her, but he didn't know Kate that well, and under normal circumstances she didn't come across as the touchy-feely type.

Sherlock appeared quicker than expected.

"Come this way," Sherlock ordered holding a side flap open.

Rafe entered first and saw the familiar slit through time. Rafe eyed Sherlock questioningly. Did Sherlock have the same powers as the Grey Guardians?

"They are waiting." Sherlock waved an arm at the portal.

Kate was a few steps behind, her feet only edging forward reluctantly. Rafe didn't fully believe she would follow him, so he grabbed her arm and dragged her.

Rafe stepped through and, once Kate was safely through also, the line sealed up behind them, and the cold, darkness of Gaul was replaced by the warmth of The Fates' house. The smell of baking itched his nose and made his mouth water.

"Rafe!" Clarence squealed from behind as two arms encompassed him. After an awkward embrace, Clarence went to also hug Kate but stopped short when he realised her arms were crossed and her head was slunk forward. "Kate, what's wrong?" When she raised her head, Clarence gasped, hand over mouth stifling any further noise. "Come with me, Kate." Clarence grabbed her by the arm and yanked her through the kitchen to the lounge area.

Anthony in his frat jacket and loincloth stood with a drink in hand by a window, peering out, at what, Rafe couldn't tell. Larissa, still as majestic as ever with her purple hair and deep purple eyes sat at a table reading a book with a half-torn spine. At their entrance, Larissa moved her book to the side. "Rafe, Kate, what's going on?"

"Sorry but I have a feeling this is urgent," Clarence said, sitting Kate next to Larissa. He grabbed a blueberry muffin and hot chocolate from the sideboard. This surprised Rafe, as it was though he was expecting them. Did Clarence know they were coming or was he always baking?

Rafe fidgeted with his hands in front while he paced.

"So, don't keep us waiting any longer, out with it then?" Anthony's gravelly voice tinged with impatience.

Rafe looked over at Kate to calculate if he should hold anything back.

"Out with it," demanded Anthony again.

"We've found out more information on who the enemy is." When in doubt, just go in and hit them hard with the truth, Rafe decided.

"How do you who it is?" Larissa's soothing voice asked.

"He was at the Battle of Alesia," Rafe said as he continued to pace.

"Are Caesar and Octavian safe?" Larissa moved forwards slightly in anticipation.

"Yes, just like Heracles was. So, whatever he came for, he got it and escaped." Rafe cast a furtive glance at Kate. "We also spoke to him before he left."

"Spoke to who? Cleon?" Anthony always wanted answers quick and fast.

He eyed Kate and opened his lips to speak, but a quiet squeak came from Kate. Everyone stared at her as she cleared her throat.

She made a deep sigh. "His real name isn't Cleon, that was a disguise, it's Sebastian," whispered Kate. "It was Sebastian."

Larissa put her hand over her mouth. "Sebastian?"

"Yes, *my* Sebastian."

Clarence's intake of breath was so loud, it made Rafe jump.

"But we presumed he had been killed, Kate?" Larissa comforted, placing a hand over Kate's.

"She's right," Rafe interjected. "The person she calls Sebastian, is the same person I knew as Cleon from Ancient Greece, and he gave me this." He raised his black tunic to reveal the Grey Guardian bracelet. "We both know him as different names, but it was him, I swear it."

"What does it mean?" Clarence squeaked.

"It means we're in big trouble." Anthony growled.

"But how can it be?" Larissa rubbed her bottom lip with her thumb. "He died."

"Technically we never found a body," Anthony answered bluntly. "So, it seems he just disappeared rather than died. What did he say to you? We need to know what he is up to."

Rafe had decided before they came to The Fates, to leave out Kate's part in almost leaving with Sebastian. It was strange referring to him by that name when he had always been Cleon to him, however the Cleon he knew had never really existed.

"When we saw him, he was next to Caesar and Octavian, but he didn't harm them, in fact, we chased him, and when we caught up with him, I realised who he was. We asked him why all the deception and what did he want, to which he said about *change* and *the lives of mortals being meddled with.*"

"And he didn't say why he was in Alesia?" Anthony was like a General taking command of a battle gone wrong, trying to make some order of it.

"No," Rafe admitted.

"Did he allude to whether he was working alone or with someone else?" Anthony persevered.

"Not that I can remember, as it happened all too quick, and I was in shock. We both were." Nodding down at Kate who had her hands wrapped around the hot chocolate, now bringing some colour back to her tear-stained cheeks.

Rafe searched the faces of The Fates for some indication of what they would do next, but what he saw scared him even more, as they looked lost for words.

Chapter Ten

Rafe laid on his bed after breakfast as he didn't feel like small talk with his family. His mind buzzed from yesterday's events. When he'd decided to come home last night after seeing The Fates, he'd flopped into bed, his body exhausted from the last few days of activity.

When he had left The Fates, Kate still sat at the table silently. Only a short time before that, she'd been the sure-footed leader of the Grey Guardians, but now he didn't recognise her. He didn't know how he felt towards her anymore.

One emotion that was in abundance though, was fear, for he knew he couldn't defeat Sebastian by himself. He would need all of the Grey Guardians to stop him, and he would need Evie, as she would know what to do. She always had the answers.

Rafe sat up, struggling to bend over from his over full stomach of two bowls of cereal and a round of peanut butter on toast. He reminded himself to eat less, like he did every day but knew he would only forget tomorrow again.

With his shoes on, he tiptoed down the stairs, then when he reached the door, he yelled out. "Off to the hospital to see Evie Mum, I'll see you later."

She replied something inaudible as he was half way out the door.

The walk to the hospital was long, as the hospital resided on the outskirts of town. Rafe found the walk allowed him to take his mind off the last events, viewing everyone's lives continued around him, oblivious to the world Rafe had discovered. At one stretch of road, he spied a small child being chased around the garden by what he presumed was a big sister. The squeals of delight coming from them both struck a chord inside of him. On another stretch he passed an old couple who held hands the whole way, and not once did they let go of each other. All around, as he made his way along the pavements, he saw people happily getting on with their lives. For them, the world continued to rotate, day after night. For Rafe though, time stood still, and not by going back in time but through the heart wrenching agony of Evie being stuck in limbo.

When he arrived at the hospital, it always amazed him how no staff stopped anyone from entering, as though trespassing into a hospital was not a possibility. The first line of security Rafe encountered was at the entrance to the ward where a locked door opened via an intercom on his side, or a green button on the other side of the door, which was visible through the lined windowpane. He pressed the buzzer and waited for the nurse on duty to let him in. Once he was led through, he waved to the other nurses as he passed them huddled around a reception desk. He'd been so often, there was no need for them to question his reasons for being there.

Turning a corner towards Evie's room, he saw a door open that led to a side room. As he walked past, he glanced inside. A female doctor was speaking to a lady with short dark hair, and although her back was to the door, he knew it was Evie's mother.

He didn't know what made him do it, but he felt the urge to stop just past the window out of sight to hear parts of the conversation.

"... as you know, your daughter is well cared for here, but it was never the long-term solution. While she isn't deteriorating, neither is she recovering. We would like to explore the option of moving her somewhere more permanent."

"Permanent?" Evie's mum questioned.

"Yes, somewhere which has the necessary high dependency equipment but offers more comfortable surroundings. This hospital isn't really suited for long term patients and we have patients coming in all the time that require intensive care. I'm not saying she needs to move yet, but there will come a time, I am afraid," the doctor said.

"When?"

"Not this week but soon after. In the meantime, how are you and your husband coping?"

Rafe didn't want to hear this bit as he could only imagine how they were feeling. He moved silently down the corridor and when he reached Evie's' room, he smiled ear to ear. The flowers he had brought some time ago were still on the side, although by the sorry look of them he wished he'd brought some more today.

On the bed, Evie lay there still as anything. A mask fixed to her face pumped oxygen into her lungs from a machine which beavered away. Tubes from her arms led up to bags of fluids hoisted above the bed and in the corner. Her diagnostics machine beeped periodically.

Once it was established, she would be in here for a long time, she'd been moved to her own room. It was a welcome relief compared to the communal ward she had initially been in.

She looked small in the bed, hooked up to all the equipment that was now her lifeforce. Although the bed cover was pulled up, he knew the wound she'd suffered was still heavily bandaged. As he'd seen it when they'd changed her dressings in front of him once. The staff had remarked at the time that it hadn't properly healed, and everyone was baffled by it.

There was a chair in the corner of the room, which had a wooden frame and a cushioned seat with backrest that was made from some wipe clean cover. Rafe thought it was a deliberate ploy by the hospital, to stop visitors from sleeping overnight as it was hard as nails.

He took his place in it and watched Evie. Processing what he had just heard, it was clear the medical staff were trying to move her somewhere else. It was true she wasn't getting better, but on the other hand, she wasn't getting worse either. She was just in limbo, teetering on a knife edge between life and death. Wherever she was moved to, he hoped it wouldn't be far as he wanted to visit her as often as he could. He hadn't expected to miss her this much, but he really did.

Oh, Evie, what are we going to do, Rafe thought, if only he knew how to heal her.

Approaching the bed, he stroked her head, moving a loose strand of dark hair out of her face. Her small heart shaped face was impassive and he longed to see her smile again.

He stood there staring at her for a long time and when his legs finally felt heavy, he left mouthing a goodbye to her.

He saw the room that Evie's mum had been in was now empty. Which made him slightly relieved, he would have hated to have had small talk with her, given he'd overheard what the doctors were planning. Where would they move her to? He wondered.

Walking out of the hospital, the weather was cloudy with sunny intervals which was pretty much a heatwave for the town. He made his way in the direction of home, but he wasn't going there. He was going to the park, where there was seating and a small stream. It was just off the main road between his house and the hospital.

All the benches were preoccupied unfortunately when he got there. He found a quiet space on the grass next to the stream and sat there, the rays of sun intermittently on his face. He allowed his eyes to shut and soak in the sun kissing his face. It was peaceful here, and his mind slowed a gear, perhaps for the first time in weeks.

How was he going to heal Evie? If only he knew a spell or had a magic potion to bring them back from the brink of death. Rafe felt his heart stop momentarily.

What had Aulus said? He used secrets from a distant tribe.

Rafe rolled names around in his head, each one nearing the mark more and more. Eventually he stumbled across a memory; Aulus had called them the Tuatha De!

Chapter Eleven

Armed with his memory from Alesia, he ran back home and paced his room. He needed to find the Tuatha De, but he had no idea where he would even start.

Taking his vial out of pocket, he placed some on his tongue. Once the vial was safely placed back in his pocket, he spread his hands in front of him and tore a hole in the fabric of space, then stepped through.

Once on the other side he found himself stood in the Great Hall of Arndell castle, tear sealed up behind him. Thankfully, the room was empty, with no guards and no Archess Silevaith on her throne entertaining guests.

As he pushed the Great Halls' doors with a grunting effort, two confused looking heads appeared from around the opening doors, their mouths wide open. The guards on the outside of the Great Hall probably hadn't accounted for intruders coming out.

"I am Rafe Stern of The Grey Guardians, take me to Megan Arndell." The wait was excruciating. "Now." His voice barely held steady.

One guard gathered her senses. She had long hair from underneath a metal helmet and an elf-like nose, sharp but flawless. "How did you get in there?" The guard's sword was not quite pointing at him but visible.

"I am a Grey Guardian, and a friend of Megan Arndell, I need to speak to her, where is she?"

The other guard piped up. "I recognise you from the other day when Archess Silevaith granted you an audience. I will stay and guard the doors, Damnia, take him to Megan."

The long blonde-haired guard grunted then strode forward. Rafe took his cue and followed. They walked different passages, then up one flight of steps and then onto a landing which had dark wooden panelling. Old curtains adorned the tall windows on the left. To the right were rooms, with no visible security, they were probably enchanted or at the very least, locked. At the third door along, Damnia knocked.

A voice came from inside.

"It is Damnia. You have a visitor, by the name of Rafe Stern."

Silence, a few steps, then the door opened.

Megan stared open mouthed. "What are you doing here, I thought the plan was for me to come to you?"

"Change of plan, I need your help." Rafe smiled.

Realising they were being watched and most likely everything being said would be reported back to the Archess, Megan dismissed Damnia.

"Come in." She opened the door wide for him to enter.

Her room was ornate and large. Her four-poster bed with red curtains jutted from the wall, and had a slight dent in it where Megan must have laid on it. A dressing table with mirror sat in front of the tall window, and the emblem of a sword flanked by wings was atop of the mirror.

"Nice room," Rafe said, and he genuinely meant it.

She rounded on him. "What are you doing here?"

"Like I said, I need your help. I've figured out a way to help Evie."

"How?" Megan said looking slightly shocked.

"The Tuatha De," Rafe said feeling elated.

"Tuatha De?" Megan queried.

Rafe repeated the story he had learnt from Aulus when he was at the Battle of Alesia. "I need to find them, as Aulus said they had the knowledge to bring people back to life."

"Where are they? How do we find them?" Megan moved to her window and began strapping a knife to her leg.

"I don't know where they are," Rafe said.

"Have you even tried to look for them? On one of your mortal devices?"

"No, not really."

Megan tilted her head to the side. "What's really going on? You could probably find them yourself so why have you really come?"

Rafe sighed. "If I'm honest, even if I find them by myself, I don't really want to go by myself. I don't know if I'll be able to get the knowledge of healing from them."

"You know, there's a war about to happen and I'm recruiting allies as well as trying to find the book."

"I know, and that's the other thing."

"Go on." Megan placed a hand on her hip.

"While I was on a mission in the timeline, we found out who is entering the timeline. It's an ex Grey Guardian, he was in the same timeline as me a few weeks back while I was protecting Heracles. And now we've seen him in the same timeline as Jupiter's son, Julius Caesar."

"That can't be a coincidence. We'll need to watch Jupiter in case he disappears as well. What was the name of this ex Grey Guardian by the way?"

"Sebastian."

"What!"

"Yeah," Rafe said a little uncertainly, "you know of him?"

"He was friendly with a lot of the shadow world, and our paths crossed a handful of times. If he's hunting for the Book of Sorothir then we're in trouble, as he knows everything about us. I don't understand why he would do this though?"

"He doesn't like how the god control and meddle with everyone's lives," Rafe summarised.

"He isn't alone in thinking that, most of the shadow world will be with him, including some angels. It's more important than ever now we prepare for war, but I don't know if we have time to find these Tuatha De. You'll have to go by yourself if it's that important." Megan made for the door,

"Megan, please help me. It won't take longer than a few hours, and then you can come straight back. Please," Rafe pleaded and contemplated going on his knees.

"The secrets of healing will still be there when the war is over." Megan shrugged.

"But what if we lose and I die. Then no one will care about Evie, and she will waste away until she dies. Give me a few hours, please." Rafe placed his hands together as though praying.

She huffed, placing both hands on her hips. "Fine. We'll need to go to my mother's private collection first though if I am to come."

They made their way down the hall, up another flight of stairs, and then passed a pair of guards who nodded to Megan. At the second door along, Megan reached for the handle and turned the gold knob.

"Isn't your mother in?" Rafe whispered.

"She's away on business, recruiting allies." The handle opened with ease and Megan pushed it open.

"That seemed easy," observed Rafe aloud.

"It's not usually. It's only because of me it opened easily. The door is protected so it'll only open by my mother's, brother's or my hand. When we were younger, my mother wanted us to be able to come and go as we please, so she extended its protection to include us. She may have a hard exterior, my mother, but losing my father and bringing up two children, all the while inheriting the title of Archess of Arndell, will do that to anyone. She had to harden herself to the outside world, but in this room, hidden away from everyone with her children playing, she could be her younger self again. Happy and carefree, those are the memories I remember of her from my childhood." Megan put the lights on, and the room lit up, revealing tapestries of angels lining the walls. By a bed was a picture of Silevaith next to a male angel. He was slender and carried an air of confidence. In their arms, was a small boy and a tiny baby. Rafe peered closer, searching to see how much change had taken place between the picture and Megan.

Megan joined Rafe's side. "My mother said that was taken just before my father died. It must be one of her last moments of complete happiness."

"How did he..." He didn't know whether he should say the word *die* or not but thankfully Megan finished for him.

"Die?" Megan paused momentarily. "During the Battle of Pieria."

Rafe had heard part of this battle from Prometheus.

Megan continued, "Arndell and the allied forces created a diversion while Sorothir showed the power of the Book and how it controlled the god. During the battle, my father was killed by Lothair, who was heir to Angelic Order Voltaire. Before he died though, my mother got retribution and killed Lothair. Afterwards she was able to hold my father in her arms as he died. I think on that day, a part of my mother died as well."

"How did she end up becoming Archess?" Rafe said, trying to piece everything together.

"My grandparents who were rulers at the time became nonchalant, the death of their son had affected them so badly. So much so, that they left for somewhere peaceful and only came back when they were ready to lay themselves to rest. In their absence, they entrusted Order Arndell to my mother who was seen as a leader by everyone after the Battle of Pieria anyway. Although my mother was not born to rule Angelic Order Arndell, she married into it and held the respect of everyone. My brother and I were too young at the time to take the position, so ever since then, she has ruled the Order, which has remained strong and safe ever since."

"Do you or your brother not want to rule?" Rafe asked.

A small laugh escaped her lips. "My brother would rule before me by birth, he also has an appetite for power. Myself though, I do not care for it as I don't like being constrained by rules and boundaries, I've seen what it's done to my mother, so I'd prefer to be a Warlord." Megan reached out and stroked the face of her father with her thumb, it was a deeply personal gesture which made Rafe feel a little sad. "Time is short so we better get on with it."

They walked through another doorway which led to a room with cabinets and books on shelves as tall as the ceiling, lining the wall from top to bottom.

"My mother's private collection of artefacts and books." Megan stepped over to a nondescript book, she pulled it out, placing it carefully on the side she reached her fingers inside.

Rafe couldn't see what she was doing but after a discernible click, Megan withdrew her hand holding a key on a leather loop. Megan took the key to a glass cabinet located by the window.

"This cabinet is protected by deadly enchantments, and to open it without the key sets off its defence mechanisms that my mother assures me are fatal," Megan said with a wink. "She doesn't remember showing me where the key was when I was really little. and I'd like to keep it that way." Opening the cabinet, Megan reached inside and gently extracted a dull grey ring with faint scratches on. "I know it looks ordinary but this ring is an ancient heirloom and has been in our family for generations. No one outside of the immediate family, has ever known that we have it, not even the rest of the members of Order Arndell."

"Why is it kept such a secret?" Rafe tilted his head to get a better view.

"Because shadow creatures, including angels, cannot just enter the timeline, time sort of pushes us out. The stronger a being is, the stronger the push is from the timeline. No offence, but that's why humans are selected to be Grey Guardians," Megan said with a sly smirk. "You're pretty powerless."

Rafe gave her a playful shove with his elbow.

"You're given power to enter the timeline by The Fates, this ring here." Megan held up a ring with red rubies encrusted around the edge which seemed to swirl and change colour as it was tilted. "It somehow harnesses their power and allows us to enter the timeline unharmed."

Rafe hadn't noticed but his eyes must have been wide with curiosity, for Megan clutched it tighter. "Don't worry, no one knows of it, and it is well guarded here."

"Is this the room your mother's part of the Book of Sorothir was stolen from?"

Megans hand went white.

"You may have a point. When we return, I'll make sure we place extra security measures in here," Megan conceded.

Rafe ran his hands along the books. "How do you suppose he got in? Sebastian, I mean, how do you think he got in here?"

"I don't know, he shouldn't have been able to." Megan frowned.

Rafe walked away from Megan pretending to scan the walls. His hand went to his chest where his secret vial of god blood was. "And how did he know about it?" Rafe couldn't help but sigh. "He's always one step ahead of us."

"Sebastian is a very resourceful person, under his guidance, the Grey Guardians were starting to regain their reputation. When he vanished, everything the Grey Guardians gained was lost with him. He built relations with our world, with races of beings who are usually seen as unworthy of entering HOG. But at this very moment, we're not on the hunt for Sebastian, are we, and I am short on time."

"Right. Evie."

Rafe stood by Megan who was eyeing some books. Megan took one out and fingered through it but after a short while, she replaced it and picked out another one.

"Yes, this is the one." Megan read a few lines in the book which was bound in brown leather.

"What is it?" Rafe asked.

"It's a historical codex, listing the names of every race, clan, tribe, group and faction of both the mortal and shadow world. It's a bit like your electrical devices but this is updated by scribes in our Order, if this Tuatha De existed then our scribes would know of them." Megan flicked page after page. "Here we are." Megan pointed to the word *Tuatha De*, in the slanted writing of one of her scribes.

"So, what does it say?" Rafe was impatient now.

Megan muttered to herself until she got half way down the page. "It says they were a supernatural race linked to an Irish god and is located in the Boyne Valley in Ireland, so if we go there during the same time as the Battle of Alesia we may find someone who can help us."

"That's amazing, Megan! Thank you!" Rafe was so overcome with happiness, he shook Megan's shoulder.

"Come on, you." Megan shirked him off.

"Hold onto me," Rafe said, "so we can enter the timeline at the same place." Rafe felt the soft touch of Megan's hand up his back and onto his opposite shoulder.

"Let's get going then."

Rafe pushed forwards with his hands, tore open a doorway and stepped through.

Rafe's foot landed in a puddle, and the clouds above were dark with rain. Rafe eyed it cautiously. Squinting in the downpour and seeing no sign of a break from the rain, he decided to run towards a large deciduous tree. Once underneath its branches, Rafe took stock of their situation.

"This is not what I had in mind," Megan spluttered, as she ruffled the water from her lank hair which was now plastered to her head. "Come over here." Megan grabbed his hand, which squelched. She pulled him to the bark of the tree, knelt down and beckoned him to do the same as well. Megan then pulled a cloak from under her armour and flung it over their heads, it almost reached the floor. It felt velvety as he rubbed the material between his fingers.

"What do we do now?" Rafe asked over the hammering of the rain.

"We wait, the clouds will blow over soon," Megan said casually, the top of her wings poking up to create a slanted roof.

"Are you sure?" Rafe replied sarcastically.

"Yes, I am sure." Megan gave a little chuckle, "I know it's hard to believe but I saw the clouds breaking in the distance.

Rafe hoped they wouldn't be crouched down like this for too long, as his legs were starting to ache. Rafe shifted his balance so that his stomach bulged outwards between his legs.

"So how are things going, searching for the book on your end?" Megan asked Rafe.

"Hmm, not very well to be honest," Rafe said feeling a little hot under the collar. "You?"

"It's hard to do much when Grainne's lacky, Nemor is always on my tail. If I don't check in with him every few days he shows up to our Castle, so I've been forced to take him with me whenever we've been asking around about the book. But no leads yet I am afraid," Megan said.

After that, Megan left Rafe to his thoughts. When he didn't think he could take any more pain and was about to stand up, he was relieved to hear the noise of the rain begin to mellow. He rose slightly from the crouch, hoping Megan would follow suit.

"It seems to have passed," Megan said to Rafe

"Good." Rafe sighed with some relief. "My knees are aching, shall we venture out?"

"Yes," Kate said.

Rafe almost threw their makeshift cover off in trying to get out and stretch his legs. Megan caught the cloak and placed it back from where she got it.

Stepping out from the cover of the tree, they surveyed their surroundings. They could see they were in a clearing next to a wood, except for the large tree that had temporality acted as their shelter, its green arms spreading wide. They were on a gentle slope which led to a small settlement.

"Shall we?" Megan indicated her arm in the direction of civilisation.

Rafe trudged along, sodden and unhappy, he hadn't prepared for this weather, and his top was soaked, raising goosebumps on his arms.

Rafe's feet squelched along the path towards the settlement, which as they got closer appeared to be a poor excuse compared to the Roman battlements he'd left behind not long ago.

This settlement used a mixture of wood of all different colours and shapes for the main entrance, then the wall was a mixture of woven reeds and briar bushes, a far cry from the sharpened palisades of Alesia. Rafe noted it was not the most secure of settlements and probably not the richest either. Drawing to within bow shot, the gate of the settlement appeared guard less, except for a small boy with a stick. At the sight of Rafe and Megan, the boy ran inside the settlement.

Walking through the makeshift gate, he saw a crudely made symbol etched into the woodwork of the arch, in the shape of a crisscross lattice. Was it a warning, or welcome?

On the other side was a wagon, which appeared to be doubled as a makeshift door to go with a makeshift gate. Once they had passed through the arch, they saw buildings, made from reeds, sticks, straw and wood.

Rafe stopped, and Megan bumped into him.

"Where to next?" Rafe queried.

"I dunno, but I'm sure a way will be presented to us."

A group of children, slightly younger than Rafe, were to one side looking at the newcomers. Megan arched her eyebrows at the sight. "Go and ask them some questions."

Realising Megan was right, and that he could use his Grey Guardian powers, Rafe shuffled tentatively up to them. They didn't have any weapons about them, but he was still a bit scared.

"Hello there," Rafe ventured.

The children stood open mouthed.

Rafe cast a look at Megan a few strides away, who just shrugged.

"I'm looking for the Tuatha De, is this the right place?" Rafe tried again.

The group of children ran off down street between buildings.

"Well that went well," Megan observed as she sidled up to Rafe. "Come on, let's take a walk."

Walking side by side through the wide street, if that's what it could be called, houses were dotted around the settlement. Wild haired owners stood in each doorway they passed. The women had their hair braided with feathers in, while the men all had scraggy beards. Most disconcerting, was that no one spoke or stopped them as they ambled down the path, they just stood and stared silently. Around a bend of houses, a tall structure came into view, with a roof made of wood and in an apex shape, while the sides were of fur and wooden slats. Stood in front of the central structure was a greying man with a beard that reached his waist. Where everyone else's clothes were dark, his was a light blue and clean with no smear marks, next to him stood the boy who had been at the gate. Behind them was a group of men and women, none of whom smiled; their hair in braids, tattoos adorned their faces and they wore weapons at their belts or in hand.

A clang of metal from behind startled Rafe and upon looking for its source, he saw a small army following them, some carried swords or axes, while others knocked arrows on their strings. "Err, Megan." Rafe elbowed Megan.

"I know, they've been following us the whole time."

"Why didn't you say something before?" Rafe could feel his knees starting to go numb.

"What would be the point? You need to help Evie, so we have to go into the lion's den," Megan said without a care in the world.

They were close to the welcoming party, so not wishing to cause any threat, Megan made Rafe stop a good distance away and waited.

The old man came a few steps forwards with two of his war party, remaining a step behind.

"Welcome," the white-haired figure said barely above a whisper. "What do we owe the pleasure of your visit?"

This time it was Megan's turn to nudge Rafe.

"We are searching for the Tuatha De," Rafe croaked out not able to take his eyes off the figure in front of him.

"And why would you seek them?" the man whispered.

"We seek knowledge to help my friend," Rafe said

"We have nothing to give here," the old man began to shuffle away.

"Tell them we can make an exchange?" Megan growled out of the side of her mouth.

Rafe gave a sideways glance but repeated what Megan said.

"Intriguing." The white-haired man shuffled back and took a step closer, staring deep into Megan's eyes and seemingly oblivious to her wings which might have been glimmered to hide their presence.

Rafe felt as though the unblinking grey eyes stared right through Megan

"This way then." He turned his back and making his way towards the structure that they stood in front of. His two guards waited for Rafe and Megan to follow then peeled behind them. Rafe noted that although their clothes were of poor quality, the furs on their shoulders marked out their status. Their hair was wild, and one of them had something long and thin interwoven into his hair. Disconcertingly they followed close behind, and Rafe cast a furtive glance back on more than one occasion.

The war party who had remained in front of the hall parted, allowing them all to travel within. Inside, furs of black browns and creams, lined the floors and walls. There was a long table in the middle with benches either side, and no surface was completely flat, giving it the feel of a living tree. The man stopped and gestured for them to sit, while he took his place at the head of the table.

"So, strangers, what information do you seek and what do you trade for it?" the grey eyed man whispered.

Rafe had noted that the man had neither agreed or denied they were the Tuatha De earlier but he had to take a risk. "I have a friend that is mortally wounded, and no matter what is applied or done, it doesn't heal, and she is barely kept alive. Then I met a soldier, a Batavian soldier who knew how to heal better than anyone else, he said the knowledge of healing had been passed to his tribe by the Tuatha De. He said that there was also knowledge of how to bring someone back from the dead, but the Tuatha De would not share that information with his tribe. I promise, I do not seek this information for any gain except to bring my friend back." Rafe unclenched his hands, not realising he had been digging his nails into his palm.

The man had his elbows on the table and his fingers intertwined.

"The knowledge of healing is not readily given to outsiders." He glanced down momentarily. "The Batavian who received it must have been a truly a remarkable person, but the sharing of such information was a mistake which our ancestors made, and not one we have made since."

"But the knowledge has helped so many people," Rafe countered.

"Perhaps, but what if our enemies get that knowledge, or this Batavian tribe became our enemy. No, we do not share our knowledge with any outsiders anymore."

"But my friend... how can I heal her?" Rafe pleaded.

"We all know someone ill or dying, I am afraid. That is what being a mortal means, our lives are easily terminated, but if you have something worthy to trade for, you can bring her to us and we can take a look at her."

"But... but..." Rafe's hand went to his pocket where Prometheus' blood was concealed. He would trade it, if there was no other way.

"That is more than we offer most. Do not push me too hard, otherwise the offer will be retracted. Now, I have taken too much time over this." He stood, waved his hand and walked towards the back of the room. "Only return here when you have something worthy to trade for."

Megan caught his eye. "Let's go," She hissed and stood at the same time to make her point clear.

"Is that it?" Rafe kept his voice down to a whisper.

Megan didn't answer as the two guards approached and stopped two strides away, an abundantly clear signal they needed to get out of there quickly.

Following Megan through the streets, he had to half jog to keep up with her large strides. Walking through the mud-strewn paths, the residents of the village stood and watched them, including one man they walked past who clenched a hammer in hand, mending something on a house.

"It didn't work," Rafe whispered. "They wouldn't give it to me."

"I know," Megan held up her hand with the ring on, "with this on I can also understand them as well as time travel. But not all is lost, at least you know where the knowledge of healing is now."

True, Rafe thought, although it was curious that Megan's ring had almost the exact same powers as a Grey Guardian.

"Just so you know, we're being watched," Megan whispered.

"The whole crazy village is watching us." He threw his arms in the air in exasperation. "Even if I do have something to trade, how am I to get Evie here?" All sort of ideas started to crop up in his head, immediately dismissed as soon as they were made.

Megan ignored Rafe and broke into a more casual voice. "I'm not ignoring you, Rafe, but there is someone following us. Don't look back!" Megan told Rafe off. "I clocked them a while back."

"Where?" He took furtive glances down every path and alley they passed, which was filled with throngs of people who watched them leave. There were more people than he had seen on his way in, it was as though they had sprung up from some hidden place.

"She's weaving in and out of the crowds. Keep moving," Megan said.

He still couldn't see anyone. "What do you suppose they want?" Rafe's pace slightly quickened.

"I don't know, but we need to get clear of this place and set up an ambush."

They were just crossing the threshold of the gateway to the village now, which still had no guard on duty. They continued down the path and passed a sparse field with a small building which might have been a farmstead. In a wooded area to the side was a large tree which was similar to the one they had taken shelter under earlier.

"Where is the person?" Rafe now cast off any illusion as he searched behind them.

"I don't know, I lost them. Hopefully that's the last we see of them though."

"*Oh really.*" A female voice came from a large thorny bush to the side, that was as stall as a door. "And what is wrong with the sight of me, may I ask?" The newcomer stepped out from behind her cover to reveal a dark-haired figure, wearing a long flowing gown. Compared to the rest of those who lived in the settlement, it was intricate and probably worth quite a bit in these parts.

Megan placed her hand on the hilt of her sword that was currently in a scabbard at her waist. "Who are you?"

"I am Princess Iseult, and I assure you, you have nothing to fear from me."

"I'll be the judge of that." Megan still kept her hand on her sword and her eyes darted all around in case anyone else was present. "Are you alone?"

"I sincerely hope so for all of our benefits, otherwise we will all be in a spot of bother, won't we," Iseult said with a sly smile.

"What do you want?" Rafe interjected, getting tired of playing games.

"Oh, don't be such a spoil sport, I was enjoying our war of words. But if you want to get down to business then, let's sit and talk." The newcomer almost seemed to glide to a fallen log close by, her dress hiding her feet.

Rafe made a move to sit beside her but Megan placed her hand on his shoulder, keeping him in place.

Megan hissed a warning, “I do not trust this one, so I suggest we keep our distance from her.”

Together, they made their way so they stood in front of Iseult, half a dozen paces away.

“I see that you do not trust me, and for good reason, I suppose. Afterall, it was my grandfather that just cast you out of his settlement.” Iseult folded her hands gently on her lap.

"Your grandfather?” Rafe said incredulously.

“He wants to marry me off to King Mark of Cornwall. Oh, that lazy old fat man.”

Rafe scowled. He thought he'd hidden his inadvertent reaction but Iseult was as observant as she appeared sly. “Oh, much larger than you,” Iseult said eyeing Rafe's middle, “ten times perhaps. I met him once and he repulses me. He had food in his beard, wine slopped down his front and lose skin hanging from his neck. I could never share a cup of wine with him, never mind be married to that oaf. No, it's his champion, Tristan, that I would like. He is dark, tall, stern looking with a few scars on his face and arms to show his valour in battle. I know he likes me, I've seen the way he looks at me.”

“So, what has this got to do with us?” Megan pointed out.

“You're looking for the Tuatha De to seek the power of healing, and I am a Princess of the Tuatha De.”

Rafe just nodded. “And I suppose you know that knowledge, do you?”

“No, they wouldn't trust me with that!” Iseult said as though it was obvious.

Rafe hadn't realised how excited he was until she had said that, he felt deflated now.

"Don't play games, Princess." Megan growled.

"I'm not playing games and I may not know the knowledge of healing, but has it ever occurred to you how the Tuatha De came about this knowledge?"

"Your grandfather did not give us the chance to ask anything," Megan answered.

"Let me strike a bargain with you. I will tell you who gave my people the knowledge of healing in return for something." Iseult raised an eyebrow as though daring anyone to question her.

"Go on," Rafe almost sighed.

"You have the means to get away from here, I presume. After all, you got here somehow?"

Rafe felt his palms sweat slightly. "We have a way out of here, yes." He needed to tread carefully on what he revealed.

"Take me to Tristan, and I will give you what you seek," Iseult said without a smile on her face, making her request all the more serious.

"No," Megan said bluntly.

Rafe snapped his head towards her, how could she make such a decision for them? This was Evie's life not Megan's.

"Hang on," Rafe ventured, "let's discuss this." He waved to the side, moving out of Iseult's earshot.

"We need her knowledge if we're to save Evie," Rafe pleased.

"She cannot know who we are and there is no way to get her off this island without you doing so. If she found out what you could do, then you could cause issues for the future.

"I won't let this opportunity bypass us. Evie's life is a good trade off to move Iseult from here to Tristan in Cornwall. It will take ten seconds, and then Evie could be saved. Her life is more important than this." Rafe placed his hands together and knew he was now begging, but he didn't care.

Megan's lips were pressed together so hard they went white. "You will need to take responsibility for what happens here, for I will not be the fall person in this. And you will need to think of a way to ensure she doesn't see you, for who you really are."

That gave Rafe a thought. "I promise she will see nothing," Rafe moved towards Iseult, who had sat with her back straight the whole time and observing their exchange.

"So?" she greeted Rafe and Megan as they made their way back to her.

"We have a deal," Rafe said

"Great!" Iseult beamed.

"But..." Rafe continued. "If I am to get you out of here then we do so on my terms, for instance, you will be blindfolded." Rafe held his hand in front of her. "Before you argue," Iseult's mouth paused half open, "we will get you there in a matter of moments, not by boat but by magic. You will be there in a split second, with no need to travel by sea, so therefore you will do it blindfolded or not at all."

"How is such a thing possible?" Iseult arched her eyebrows.

"Magic." Rafe felt the corners of his mouth twitch slightly.

"Magic?" Iseult repeated.

"Yes, magic. Come then, let's get this started."

Princess Iseult stepped forwards, her hips swaying as she crossed the ground.

"Pass me that." Rafe pointed at Iseult's waist where a small pieced of material was being used for a belt.

"This?" Iseult grabbed the material to make her point.

"Yes, I need to blindfold you. If we are going to do this, you cannot see how we get there, okay?"

Iseult shrugged her shoulders and undid the knot at her waist, handing the material to Rafe.

Rafe spun her around and spread it across her eyes, tying the knot firmly. When he was done, he guided her towards Megan.

"Are you sure you want to do this?" Megan questioned Rafe again.

His hand was still on the knot. "Yes, I do."

Rafe took Iseult's hand in his left, it was slender, and rougher than he was expecting and he placed it on his shoulder. At the same time, he felt Megan's hand on his other shoulder.

"So," Rafe called over his shoulder to Iseult. "Where does Tristan live?"

"Close to Castle Dore, he owns a minor settlement there."

"Hold on," Rafe said, feeling a gentle squeeze on his shoulder.

Placing his hands together, he thrust forwards, saw the familiar tear, opened it wider and took a step. On the other side, it was much like where they had been; cold, damp and muggy. The only difference was the coast, with the sea whipping in front of them and the taste of salt in the air, which he breathed in savouring the taste and smells. A small palisaded settlement was close by and in the distance was a castle.

"We're here," Rafe declared. Megan let go, but Iseult who was still blindfolded, kept her hand on Rafe's shoulder. Removing it gently, then lifted the makeshift blindfold from Iseult's face so she could see their surroundings.

Iseult gasped loudly. "How is this so?"

"We told you," Megan said a little impatiently. "Magic. Now unless you want to go back, tell us what we bargained for."

"You are looking for the Goddess Airmed, she taught my people the gift of healing and how to bring people back from the dead." Iseult ran her hands through her hair.

"Airmed?" Megan asked, "You're sure?"

Iseult snorted. "I have no need to lie, I do not care what befalls the Tuatha De and their scheming with my life."

"Have you heard of her?" Rafe quizzed Megan hopefully.

Megan just shook her head. "Not here," she hissed.

"How will you find her, by the way, she is a goddess," Iseult questioned.

Rafe ignored Iseult and scanned around, there was a large rock formation behind them near the cliff edge. Placing the material in his pocket, he pointed with his chin in the direction of the rocks. "Let's go over there," he suggested to Kate.

"Good idea, I need to get back." Megan made her way towards them.

Before Rafe joined Kate, he looked at Iseult. "For what it's worth, good luck with whatever lays ahead for you. Thank you." Rafe wasn't sure if she deserved his thanks, but he couldn't help it, he was always apologising or thanking someone. He followed Megan and heard Iseult shout after him.

"How will you find her?" Iseult's voice strained against the wind which swept her thin dress about her ankles, threatening to pull her over.

"Magic," Rafe called back with a beaming smile before he rounded the stone formation.

Megan was there waiting, she had opened a tear in time, and she held it open, her hand outstretched. He took it, and she pulled him through.

No doubt Iseult would have followed them around the corner, but all she would find would be bare rocks.

They were now back in Silevaith's private library. Rafe found a seat and slouched in it, feeling a bit damp still from the rain.

"Airmed," Rafe played the word along his tongue. "Airmed. Where do you suppose we look for her?"

"HOG I guess," Megan said.

"So, you haven't heard of Airmed?" Rafe queried.

"I know of the name but I haven't met her before. I suggest you start there though."

"At HOG? Me? Do you mean you aren't coming?" Rafe sat upright.

"I can't, I'm afraid. Now we know Sebastian is working against us, our situation is even more perilous. I must go to the shadow creatures to ensure our tenuous alliances do not waver." Rafe busied herself making sure her mum's room was as they had found it.

"But how... what will I... I mean, I don't know the first thing about where to look," Rafe said feeling lost.

"I'm sorry, but I'll help you after I get back."

"And how long will that take?" Rafe bit back, clenching his fists.

"I don't know in all honesty. Two days, maybe three, it depends on how desperate our situation is." Megan placed her mother's most treasured possession back in the protected cabinet.

"What about the Book of Sorothir? Have you got any further leads on it?" Rafe asked

"No. You?"

"None." Rafe sighed, "not yet I am afraid."

"I have no doubt that Sebastian knows where they are. He wouldn't have made his move if he did not know." Megan placed the key back in its secret location.

"So, we wait until he makes his move then." Rafe waved his arms in the air.

"What else can we do? I'm sorry, but we must part ways now, I'd show you out, but as you have the power to come and go as you, please, there seems little point really." Megan strode purposefully towards the door. "I truly am sorry I can't help more at the moment. I hope you find what you are looking for, Rafe." With that, she left, and the door closed behind her.

Surveying the room, he would have loved to have searched the place to find its hidden treasures. But the knot in his stomach reminded him of his need to bring Evie back and the idea of finding treasures would be more of a chore. With nothing left to do, he opened a tear in time back home.

Chapter Twelve

Rafe hadn't felt the need to go home yet so instead, he walked to a small newsagents close to his house. Walking inside, there was the usual newspapers of the day on the shelf next to the door, then two islands of shelves lined the middle of the shop, while the perimeter walls were adorned with a mixture of fridges. He wheeled towards the counter, picked up a chocolate bar, and paid the attendant behind the counter.

He was barely out of the door, when he ripped off the wrapper and placed the rubbish in his pocket. As he ate his bar, he walked the pavements, passing rows of houses and parked cars, keeping an eye on where he placed his foot. The area was known for dog excrements, perhaps it was a stray or just one inconsiderate owner. Which was a shame as the dogs he passed on his walk, all seemed lovely, and the owners always offered a friendly smile.

He walked around aimlessly, treading down streets he hadn't been down before, finding hidden places of tranquillity. He passed a high wooden fence, which ended with an open parkland. He headed towards a small pond, hidden in a corner, amidst the green expanse. There were some small benches overlooking it but all were occupied except one, which he headed towards.

Taking in the surroundings, he saw an older couple on one bench and on another. a young couple watching their two children dangle long pieces of grass into the pond. Rafe thought they might be brother and sister, having the same sandy coloured hair, they giggled together as they bobbed their long pieces up and down over the water.

It made Rafe smile at the sweet innocence and happiness of them. Such simple games they were playing, which brought them immeasurable joy. It was moments like this, seeing the older girl and younger boy playing together, that made him think of the times he and his sister, Kira, had once been close, but age, school and his lack of popularity had driven that apart. Did it happen to all siblings or was it just the unique circumstances of his sibling bond?

He closed his eyes and raised his head to the sky, the heat of the sun warming his eyelids. He sighed, knowing that he was only allowed a moment of relaxation. Placing his hand in his pocket, he felt the familiar shape of Iseult's belt, as he fingered it, he wondered why he had placed it in his pocket at all. One thing for sure though, was the material reminded him of the one person he needed right now, which was Airmed. And even finding her would not guarantee a cure for Evie, though sitting here would guarantee she wouldn't have any cure. He didn't even know where to look in HOG, just asking a round like a weak human wouldn't get anyone to co-operate. He needed help, and perhaps he should wait for Megan, it would certainly be a sensible and safe option.

With some effort, he stood up, and watched a dragonfly hover over the pond. Somewhere he had read that a dragonfly only lived for a few weeks. Rafe decided that if he were a dragonfly, he'd think this would be a nice place to live out the few weeks of his existence, buzzing around the reeds of the pond.

He walked leisurely back home, kicking stones as he went, scuffing the toes of his shoes. His mother would kill him if he made holes in them.

Before he knew it, his feet had taken him to the front of his house of their own accord. Finding the key to his house from the depth of his pocket, he hadn't realised that evening was approaching.

With a heavy sigh, he opened the door, knowing that his parents and sister Kira would be going about their lives like normal, oblivious to what was happening beyond this world. Their small problems massive to them but in reality, meaningless. They would go on like this all night, all the while, he would feel helpless inside.

It felt like his head had only just hit the pillow before he was being shaken.

"Wake up!"

He recognised the voice and opened one eye as wide as it would go. "What?" Rafe croaked into the darkness of his room.

"Wake up, it's school and we're leaving in fifteen mins," Kira said.

"School?"

"It's Monday, dummy." Rafe heard Kira close the door and her footsteps move down the hallway.

He'd forgotten about school. It had been half term last week, and he had completely forgotten about his real life. Which seemed trivial compared to the events of the last few days. Perhaps he could time travel to avoid school, but where would he go and what would he do? He couldn't time travel in

HOG, that was one place his powers wouldn't work. The Fates said time doesn't exist there which meant you couldn't go back or forwards. Events happened and they couldn't be changed, so he couldn't go back in time to stop Sebastian throwing the knife outside HOG. He'd contemplated the idea of going further back, to a time before Sebastian became a Grey Guardian but he would have to discuss that with Kate to find out why no one had suggested it.

"Rafe! Ten minutes!" his mum called up, bringing him out of his thoughts.

"Oh, shoot." Rafe put his PE kit on, which was placed neatly on a chair in his room by his parents. When Rafe ran downstairs, he grabbed some toast with peanut butter and followed his sister to the car, which their mum had already loaded with their school bags.

The drive to school was painful. It always was in the morning. His mum usually tried to ask trivial things, like how they both were? What they planned on doing today? What plans they had with their friends? Which was usually a conversation killer for him as he didn't have any friends apart from Rory. Kira though, had an abundance of answers to all the questions and as she talked, it occurred to Rafe that she seemed to have a friend named for every type of flower.

At the school gates, Rafe's mum explained she had a meeting, and his dad would be picking him up later.

After they entered the school gates, Kira said bye quietly, leaving Rafe to walk alone, while she was embraced by an armful of her friends.

Even though Rafe thought most of Kira's friends were the fake sort, it must be nice to be welcomed every morning as though you were a long-lost friend. Rafe grudgingly admitted he would have liked that, even by friends that were fake.

Walking into the school, he resolved to get through the day without incident so he could spend more time this evening, on solving his problem of going to HOG to find Airmed.

For the most part, Rafe found himself moving from lesson to lesson like a zombie. It was uneventful, until PE at the end of the day. As they were in PE kit there was no need to get changed, they just went out in the clothes they had on. They were learning different sports from the Olympics; triple jump, high jump, shot put, 100 metre sprint, all the sports you could do on grass, as the school had no athletics track. He found himself in the top three for shot put, which he was pleasantly surprised about. Those fighting reps must have helped, Rafe mused. He also found himself moving up from the usual last place in the 100m sprint, to the lower-middle of the pack, which although he still received abuse for, it wasn't as nearly as much as usual.

"Well done, tubby," one class member retorted as a backhanded compliment.

"Did you roll yourself over the line?" Someone else said to laughter from the others.

For the most part, Rafe ignored them, except when one of the boys tried to pull his shorts down, saved only by the extra tight knot Rafe had tied that morning, Rafe felt his anger start to bubble. Rafe pictured himself pushing the boy backwards, standing up for himself, which probably would have ended with him being sent to the headmistress. Instead, he fell to his default position of remaining quiet and gently shoulder barging his way out of the group towards the edge of the mingling crowd.

What would Evie have done if she were here? Would she had said something or would she have stood silently by his side in quiet support?

At the end of the day, Rafe's dad greeted him with a welcome hug. Rafe liked it when his dad hugged him, the arms fully ensnaring Rafe in a warm embrace with no room to wriggle free. It was reassuring and Rafe knew it held a lot of love.

The car journey home was uneventful and finding himself tired, Rafe closed his eyes momentarily. When he walked into the house, Rafe could smell the familiar aroma of his mum's lasagne which she had left on the side before going to her meeting. Rafe's mouth watered from the smell. He loved her lasagne, which was all homemade except for the sauce; some people liked to make their sauce from scratch but nothing beat lasagne sauce from a jar.

Rafe remembered that his homework today was reading, a nice simple task which is how he liked it. He took the book upstairs to his bedroom and laid on his bed, opening the book to the first chapter. Despite his enthusiasm to start his work, the words seemed to bypass his brain. School was nothing compared to the Battle of Alesia. Which was a thought process that distracted him even more, as he wondered where Kate was.

Kate! He sat up in bed. She could help as she knew HOG and would know where to start looking for Airmed.

Rafe got onto the internet and searched for Kate McNulty. After an hour of trying to find her, he threw his arms in the air and opened his window for some cool breeze. Whatever he searched for, he couldn't locate her, for all intents and purposes, she did not exist.

Rafe sat in front of the computer again and felt his head begin to droop. He allowed it, knowing he was exhausted. His eyes shut, and as his mind began to swirl into the fog of dreams, he jerked awake.

"Stalking me, are you?" Someone called from behind.

"What!" Rafe spluttered and sat up.

Kate, with wavy hair in a pony tail and wearing jeans and a t-shirt pointed to the screen behind Rafe. He cringed inside as he saw Kate's name on the computer.

"I was trying to find you," Rafe said, feeling flustered. "I wasn't stalking you, I promise."

"Sure." Kate dragged out and smiled.

"I wasn't, I promise. Besides why are you here?"

"I like to check up on our new recruits every now and then. Making sure you're still on board."

Rafe cocked an eyebrow. "Well, as you can see, I am."

"Good. So, why were you looking for me?"

Rafe inhaled deeply. "I wanted to find where you were because I need you." Rafe noted his voice had gone high pitched. "I've found a way to bring Evie back, and I need to go to HOG, except I don't really know HOG so I needed someone to guide me."

"And you think I can help?" Kate placed her hand on her chest.

"Yes, I have no idea about HOG and you do." Then something occurred to Rafe, "Why are you here anyway, and how did you know where I live?"

"I know where all the Grey Guardians live, and you couldn't find me as I like to keep a low profile online, you never know who is watching you. But I came to see how you are doing, being a newbie isn't easy, and we're a bit thin on the ground so we could do with you sticking around to help us."

"Of course, I'm sticking around," Rafe declared as though it was obvious. "But I do want to help Evie first though."

"You like her, don't you?" Kate said with her head cocked.

No one had really asked him this. Now that he had to think about it and answer it, he didn't know what to say. "It's my fault she is in this situation, and if I don't bring her back, I'll never forgive myself."

"I get you, Rafe." Kate smiled from ear to ear. "And for the record, I know you're in love with her."

"I'm what!" Rafe bit back, feeling himself go red.

"Whatever, but I know what I can see. So, HOG. where abouts?"

"To find Airmed."

Chapter Thirteen

Rafe surveyed his surroundings which seemed to be an alleyway in HOG.

"Where is this alleyway located precisely?" Rafe asked.

"Next to The Silent Chamber," Kate pulled his arm. At the mouth of the alley, they came out into a beautiful forecourt with pink flowers climbing the buildings. One building with steps leading up to it dominated the area and had large wooden doors with metal all around it. A few angels and god who were present in the forecourt, passed the steps the steps of the building in front.

"What's The Silent Chamber?" Rafe said in wonder, as he took in the dozen steps that led up into an ornate building.

Kate strode past the building in the direction of the hall that was the centre of HOG.

"It's where important artefacts are kept and is the most secure building in HOG, which makes it the most secure place in the world. Nothing escapes it, and no one can break in."

"Wow, what's it like in there?" They made their way up a path, lined with gravel, which was wide enough for them to pass those that came down the hill.

"I don't know to be honest. All I know is that it's guarded by seven angels all day and night, who remain silent the entire time, one angel from each of the angelic orders," Kate said as she effortlessly bounded up the path.

"The same angel guards it day and night or do they have a rota?" Rafe asked breathlessly.

Her head twisted around, and she cocked an eyebrow. "How do I know, I've never been in."

Rafe felt as though Kate's strides were getting longer as his breath laboured further. He placed his hands on his legs to propel himself forward with each step, while his breathing rasped in his lungs. When Rafe reached the top, Kate was waiting for him.

She had the courtesy to say nothing and just shook her head. "This way," she said, bounding onwards, without allowing Rafe any respite.

"So... where... will... Airmed... be?" Rafe asked in between breaths.

"From what you say, she is a Celtic god of healing and she uses herbs as part of the process. Based on that, I think it's prudent to start looking in the forest past the Angel Gardens."

"The what?" Rafe frowned.

"You say that a lot you know. The Angel Gardens, it's a place where angels go to remember their dead, and is full of tall hedges, wild flowers and monoliths. A wild wood borders the edge of it, which I haven't been to before, but I've heard that some of the more pagan-esque god hang out there, to be closer to nature. Come on, let's get going."

With Kate leading the way, they circled HOG, going around the back of the building to a sea of greenery and bright colours.

"Wow," Rafe couldn't help himself say, it was simply stunning.

"Impressive, isn't it?" Kate said with a smile, "I remember the first time I saw it as well."

The grass was a piercing green and tall hedges lined the entirety of the gardens, some were neat in places and others jagged. The pattern of which unfolded the more he stared. In the centre of the green sea were white monoliths, an eerie haze of blue and green drifted up from them, as though the heat created a mirage. The further you got from these tall structures of beauty, which could only be made of stone presumably, the untidier the bushes and flowers got, as though the wild was battling with order. A war that took place slowly and underfoot from the number of figures that dotted about the sea of green.

"Are they angels?" Rafe nodded to the figures that moved about the gardens.

"Yes," Kate said as she made her way down to an entrance marked by two white columns of white stone that were smooth to the eye with no ridges. "It is one of the few places that they are not allowed to quarrel. See here." She pointed to something inscribed on the column, indiscernible.

"What does it say?" Rafe arched his neck to see it in its entirety.

"I don't know but this inscription is imbued with ancient magic and no angels in my lifetime have defied the rules for me to find out what happens if anyone breaks them and quarrels." They walked through, the grass interspersed by single pebbled paths that criss-crossed in different directions.

"So, you're saying basically, don't start any fights?" Rafe gave a slight snigger.

"You've got it," Kate agreed.

"But out of the two of us, I reckon you're the one most likely to cause a fight," Rafe said with a slight smile.

To which Kate barked a rare laugh.

They headed adjacent to where all the paths seemed to lead, in the direction of an area where the tallest trees overlooked the Angel Gardens.

As they weaved through, he couldn't help but marvel, open mouthed, at the colours of flowers that seemed to appear in every nook and hedge, they were of the most vivid and brightest he had ever seen. His eyes were drawn to one group of flowers made up of yellow and pinks, which he slowed to take a better look.

"If only I had a camera," Rafe whispered to himself.

Kate who had taken a few steps forward pivoted on her heel to see what had caught his attention. "These are my favourite." Her fingers lightly touched the petals of a flower that was at one moment, pink, the next purple and then blue. They shimmered with the wind and sun. "I used to think they were magical flowers." She rubbed her fingers along the flower and a powder was left on her fingers, which also shimmered. "Beautiful, isn't it? I used to come here a lot."

Rafe noted a tear slide down her cheek, making its way down to the ridge of her jawbone, before falling onto one of the flowers below, causing the rainbow powder to smudge. Rafe wondered if he should say something. Instead, he settled on resting a hand on her shoulder as he walked past. "Come on."

Rafe walked through the hedges, hoping he was going in the right direction, until eventually Kate drew alongside. He had to admit he was relieved she steered them to their destination, as he didn't have a clue which way to go.

Feet crunching on the stones below that marked paths via white pebbles, they headed to a gap in the hedges that led to a thick forest. It reminded Rafe of something from a sinister wood he'd seen in a cartoon in his youth. When he reached the threshold, he saw the same white pillars with markings on, but it wasn't them that caused him to hesitate crossing the invisible boundary. The gnarled-looking trees in front, with their bends and twists, told him all he knew, this was a very old and wild wood.

Kate was a few strides ahead before she noticed Rafe was left behind. She held her hand out. “Come on, Rafe. It’s safe, this is all part of HOG.”

Rafe didn’t take her hand, thinking it would have been weird, instead he nodded to her as he drew beside her. “Do you know where you are going?” Rafe queried.

“I haven’t been here before but I guess we follow this path,” Kate said as she pointed at the floor.

Until Kate had pointed to it, Rafe hadn’t noticed the trampled foliage and worn grass until now. This path was a lot better hidden, compared to the pebbles of the Angel Garden.

“Ladies first.” Rafe gestured with his arm.

“I don’t believe in that rubbish,” Kate said.

And Rafe believed her.

“But I’ll go first as I know you’re scared.” Kate smirked and moved ahead, but before she passed, she beamed at him, the first time in a while she had done that. He didn’t mind admitting that her words were true,

They made their way through the wood, which was hard going and they had to stop on one occasion so Rafe could catch his breath. Kate didn’t need the break, as she knew Rafe wasn’t as fit as her.

Eventually, they came across hidden cuts at the base of old trees. A trickle from a nearby stream could be heard, along with the chirping of birds as they scoured the forest floor for grubs.

Rafe had an overwhelming sense of being watched throughout the trek, which was only too soon confirmed to Rafe, as a tree next to them moved. Or, more accurately, a man with a green face and beard, which appeared more like moss and dead grass, came away from a tree.

The tree man stumbled forward unbalanced, and Rafe took a step back. He wasn't ashamed to let Kate deal with him and run if necessary.

"What is your... purpose here?" It rasped slowly.

Rafe eyed him up and down trying to determine whether he was more tree or man, and not coming up with a definitive answer.

"Ancient god of our time, we have come to see Airmed," Kate declared with a bow of her head and an air of confidence which Rafe could never muster.

Rafe found the salutation curious though, especially as Kate had said ancient god of our time.

"And what is your... purpose with her?" The treeman swayed slowly.

"We seek her wisdom, ancient god of our time."

The treeman took a step back into the tree it had come from, blending back into the space. Before he closed his eyes, he raised his arm pointing.

Rafe cast a glance to where it directed, where a hut sat by a stream. When Rafe tried to find the Greenman again, the arm of the ancient god had now become a branch and his eyes were almost invisible, only the trained eye saw the hint of an outline.

Kate was eyeing Rafe and nodded in the direction they had been instructed to go.

When Rafe determined them to be a safe distance, he leaned into Kate. "What was that?"

"That was one of the oldest god around," Kate answered as she stepped over a bush that lay in their path, small red flowers protruded but underneath the flower heads were a small ring of thorns.

"What was his name?" Rafe asked as he carefully stepped over the bush.

"I'm not going to make it that easy, let me give you a clue. He's associated with the month of May and you will find his face on a garden wall as an ornament." Kate brushed a line of leaves that circled a tree branch like ivy, but at her touch, the leaves took flight.

Butterflies swirled around them and flew off into the tree canopy above.

Rafe had to admit he wasn't entirely sure of the answer but knew he had one at home; a stone man's face framed by leaves, like a lion's mane. "Ah I think we have one in our garden but I don't know what it's called."

"He's called the Greenman and he is a very old god, who is able to hide amongst any tree."

They appeared close by the hut at the water's edge. A young lady who was in her early twenties with wavy orange hair, sat stroking the water causing ripples to disperse from her fingertip.

The snap of a twig under Rafe's clumsy foot broke the spell, and the young lady's face snapped towards them, which held a deep scowl.

"Who dares disturb the tranquillity around us?" the orange-haired figure said. Then at seeing Rafe and Kate, her frown seeming to deepen even more. "Mortal, it seems, not even shadow creatures."

"What do we do?" Rafe panicked.

"Go down to see her." Kate shrugged.

"Is that wise?" He really didn't know what would happen if they did.

"She's a god. Even if we ran away, we wouldn't stand a chance, so it's best to just confront it head on." Kate went to move down to the water.

"Kate." Rafe warned reaching out an arm to stop her.

"Yes?"

"Is there any part of you that is as scared as me?"

He hadn't seen this expression on her before, pursed lips and her face creased in concentration. "I'm slightly scared, to be honest." Despite that though, Kate ambled down to the stream as though there was no care in the world. How she kept her nerves was impressive to watch.

Rafe had to pry his legs from the spot, seemingly stuck in place.

Once they reached the edge of the water, Rafe noticed the skin of the orange haired figure was completely blemish free, her hair wavy as though she had just been for a swim. She wore a pure white dress that reached the floor, around the next a ring of pearls was embroidered.

The lady eyed Rafe up and down, making the hairs on the back of his neck stand on end.

"I thought you were going to run for a second, which would have been awfully embarrassing for you once I caught you." The lady stood up and stared them down.

Rafe caught the corner of Kate's eye, wondering if she had overheard the conversation Rafe just had about running away.

"So out with it then, who are you and why are you sullying our forest with your presence?"

"Rafe," Kate whispered and beckoned a hand for him to answer.

Rafe felt as though he was being thrown under a bus but then again it was his idea to find Airmed.

"Are you Airmed?" Rafe said meekly.

"Do I look like Airmed to you?" The wavy-haired lady said.

"I... I don't know what Airmed looks like?" Rafe admitted openly.

The god before them scowled and crossed her arms. It was evidently the wrong thing to say. "What I mean to say is, I have never seen Airmed before, but if I had to imagine what she looked like, it would be as someone graceful like you."

That brought a light laugh, strands of orange hair falling over her face, and her hand covering her mouth to stifle further laughter. "You are funny for a mortal, aren't you? Come." The lady beckoned and silently walked across the moss beaten path to a log a little further down the bank. As she made her way to it, the tip of her toes poked out from the edge of her dress.

She picked up a mortar and pestle that was resting on the log and began to grind it.

"So, what of it then? Who are you, and why are you here to see me?"

So, she was Airmed, Rafe felt elated that he had found the person who might be able to help him.

"Out with it quickly, I don't have all day," she commanded with a slight edge to her voice.

"My name is Rafe, and this is Kate, we are Grey Guardians." He waited for her to respond but she continued to grind away with the contents in the mortar. Rafe ploughed on, "I have been on a long journey to find the knowledge of healing."

"And what makes you think I know of such knowledge?"

"Because you once shared such knowledge with the Tuatha De," Rafe said with a little too much smugness that made his cheeks redden.

The mortar stopped momentarily but started again as quickly as it had stopped. "Ah, so you met them, have you? How do they fair?"

"Erm, perhaps a little guarded, I guess," Rafe said not knowing how else to describe the cold reception he had received.

"And so, they should be." She stopped the pestle and took the contents of the mortar to a bowl, which she tipped the contents into, she then mixed it in with her finger, then dipped three cups into it. Placing one beside her seat, she handed the other two to Rafe and Kate.

Kate sniffed it and wrinkled her nose. "Thank you, Airmed."

"It is a drink of elixir that will remove any ailments you have." She took a sip of her own to show it was safe.

Kate put the cup to her lips.

Airmed sat and watched in silence, as though waiting for something to happen. When nothing did, she continued with a shrug of the shoulders.

"So why is it two Grey Guardians seek knowledge of healing? Not that you will get it from me."

"It's for my friend Evie. She isn't a Grey Guardian, but she was struck by a knife, here." Rafe indicating the place it had gone through Evie. "She's stabilised but remains in... limbo. Nothing is making her better, in fact, her wound is still bleeding and it's been weeks now."

Airmed tapped the cup in her hand. "I doubt any ordinary healing potion would work on her."

"But you taught the Tuatha De the power to revive those from the dead, which they guard closely." Rafe squeezed his palms together, trying to dissipate his anxiety, he didn't know which way this conversation would go.

"Whoever told you that, my dear, must have been playing a trick on you. All I know are simple tricks to heal, not how to bring people back from the dead. If there were such a power then there would be a lot of corpses walking about, believe me," Airmed said.

Rafe's body went numb. Airmed was his final thread of hope, and it had been dashed. What was he to do now?

He wanted to ask her more questions, but his mouth wouldn't work. An arm draped around his shoulders and he felt hair tickle his face as he was guided off the log, one step and then another.

"No," Rafe whispered. "No!" Rafe shouted louder. Rafe noted Kate's nervous glances towards Airmed, who tugged a little harder at Rafe, but he spread his legs into a wide base with knees bent. "There must be a way, you are an ancient god of healing. If there is a way, you must know it."

Airmed's face morphed into a picture of anger. "How dare you speak to a god like that. You do not come here and tell me what to do, I could kill you in an instant you little ..."

"Come on, Rafe." Kate yanking his arm, the time for subtlety vanished.

"She knows something, and I have to help Evie," Rafe pleaded not caring what Airmed did to him.

"Rafe, she will kill us both. Please..." Kate grabbed his arm in both of her hands and yanked, causing him to skid across the ground.

"Insulant children." Airmed waved her hand and a green shimmering wall sprung up blocking them from Airmed. Rafe's fingertips touched it, making his fingers instantly recoiled, feeling as though he'd been stung by nettles.

Airmed moved away from them down the stream. "Leave now and you may live to see another day."

"Let her go," Kate growled towards Rafe, pinning him in place to stop him following. "You don't want a god's wrath aimed at you."

Rafe struggled with less effort.

When Kate eventually released him, he felt a bruise on his chest, rubbing it, his hand brushed against a lump in his pocket.

"What's up?" Kate asked, surveying the force field that Airmed had created.

"You have a tight grip."

"Come on, I didn't hold you that tight. Besides, that barrier Airmed created will be impenetrable, there's no way you will be able to speak to her again."

Rafe dipped his hand into his pocket, suddenly remembering what the lump in his pocket was. Prometheus' blood! Knowing Kate would disagree, he turned his back on her, dabbed a drop on his lips, tasted it and then thrust his arms out.

Stepping through the tear, he gazed back at Kate. Should he tell her or leave her? He knew he'd be pretty upset if he'd been left, so he held the tear open a little longer and shouted.

"Kate!"

A picture of confusion spread across her face. "How?"

"No time, you coming or what?" He stepped through holding the last bit of the gap open enough for Kate to step through behind.

They found themselves not having time travelled but having moved through space to a position that was in front of Airmed, who ambled towards them and eyed a butterfly hovering by a bush with pink flowers.

"Airmed," Rafe called out with as much confidence as he could muster. He felt Kate stepping in behind him, thanking her inwardly that she said nothing.

"How did you bypass the barriers, no one should be able to?" Shock creeping into Airmed's voice.

"A gift from a friend," Rafe said simply.

"Which friend?" Airmed took a step forward.

"Prometheus," Rafe admitted.

Aimed stopped mid-step, tossed her head back and chuckled. "You know Prometheus?"

"Yes." He knew it wasn't entirely true as he had only met him once. Although on that one occasion he had saved Prometheus, he wouldn't have described them as friends but Airmed wasn't to know that.

"You've met him?" Airmed smiled.

"Yes. What is it with all the questions?" Rafe wondered aloud.

"I'm just surprised that you have travelled to Tartarus to see Prometheus."

"Well, he's not there anymore," Rafe said with a smirk. He then felt a nudge at the bottom of his back, Kate was warning him of something.

"Oh really, do tell." Airmed grinned widely, having lured him into her trap.

"I set him free. He needed help and, in return, he gave me a gift to bypass any barrier," Rafe said.

Airmed stood staring at Rafe. He tried to work out what she was thinking, as he couldn't read her. Finally, she waved her hand in the air and the protective wall down the path vanished. Airmed then walked back the way she had come to her shelter.

"Come then," Airmed declared over her shoulder, the strands of her orange hair flicking over her shoulder.

Rafe eyed Kate, who gave a shrug, so he followed Airmed.

They meandered away from the river towards a hut, which was topped with straw and made with bamboo. All around, climbing flowers of pink and yellow blossomed.

It was strange walking along that path, it was tranquil with only the sounds of insects buzzing away, animals foraging on the ground and birds rustling in the trees. But there were occasions when he thought he saw a shadow of a person hiding behind trees. The image of the Greenman came to the fore, if there were two gods in these woods there were certain to be many more. Were they watching them now?

When they finally reached the log again, Airmed sat cross legged with her hands in her lap.

"So, you set Prometheus free?" Airmed asked again.

"Y... Yes." Rafe couldn't figure out what she was thinking, and it unnerved him.

She stood and clapped his hands. "He's left Tartarus then, perfect. And what gift did he give you to bypass barriers?"

"His..." Rafe didn't want to reveal his secret but the raised eyebrow of Airmed, left Rafe with no doubt he had no choice in the matter. "Blood, he gave me some of his blood."

"He gave you what!" Kate blurted out, rounding on him. "Show me now!"

Rafe tentatively showed the small vial of red liquid from his pocket but made sure he kept a firm grip on it, in case anyone tried prying it away. When he felt he had shown them long enough, he snatched his arm back and placed the vial inside his pocket.

"Why on earth did you set him free?" Kate asked, rounding on him. "I thought you were bluffing back there?" Pointing back the way they had come.

Rafe tried to think of a good excuse but not able to think of any which didn't sound lame, he took a deep breath.

"He needed help," Rafe said earnestly.

"He needed help! Did it not occur to you that he was put there for some reason. That whoever put him there would not be happy when they discovered he had been released and by no other, than a Grey Guardian?"

It had occurred to him, and the thought of a god tying to exact revenge on him was enough to keep him awake at night sometimes. But all that worry was put to bed, when he reminded himself that he couldn't deny that his gift was proving useful.

Kate closed her eyes and took a deep intake of breath.

Rafe hadn't noticed that Airmed silently crossed towards them to watch the drama unfold. Her red hair, with the light shining down on it, looked like fire as she stood next to them.

"How much blood did he give you?" Airmed asked, causing Kate's eyes to open suddenly.

Reluctantly, he took the vial out again and showed it to both of them.

"He gave you a lot, that is some gift! And to pass the barrier I created, you placed some in your mouth, correct?"

Rafe nodded.

Airmed placed her hand under Rafe's and forcibly closed his hand around the vial. Airmed's soft hand tingled, as though it was charged with static.

"You know, rather than taking a sip each time you require it, if you drink it in one go, you will have the power for life," Airmed said, removing her hand from his.

Rafe rubbed the back of his hand, still feeling the after effects of Airmed's touch.

"Will I, how do you know?" Rafe stammered out.

"Because I have bestowed my blood as a gift to someone before. It is rare for a god to do so, but the recipient then receives unimaginable gifts. Prometheus always had a gift of getting past places that were seemingly impossible to cross, it's how he stole fire for man. No one else could have done that. I, have the power to heal for instance." Airmed nodded and some loose strands of her orange hair fell across her eyes.

Rafe felt the burning question inside him bubble up, he needed to know if it was possible. "Do you have the power to... bring people back from the... dead?" Rafe finally managed.

She cocked her head to the side, as though peering into his soul.

"Prometheus saw something in you. He is a principled god, and we were once part of something a long time ago, it was a cause that I believed in passionately. We both did, along with many others. If he trusts you then so will I. So, yes," Airmed said. "I can bring people back from the dead."

There it was. Rafe's heart leapt, and he tried to breathe, but no air would come in. He took a small breath to alleviate the dizziness, and his legs went to jelly. Thankfully, strong arms grabbed him from behind.

"Breath, Rafe. Breath." Kate's hot breath brushed his cheek.

The enormity of finding what he'd been searching for was overbearing.

Rafe tried to take in some air, which came in sparingly. Kate lowered him to his knees and two blurry figures passed into view.

"Breath, Rafe," Kate repeated.

Now that he'd found a way to bring Evie back, would Airmed give that knowledge to him? Cold air rushed into his lungs.

"That's it Rafe, take another breath," Kate said.

Now that Airmed had admitted she had the power to save Evie, she would not deny him the chance to bring her back now, surely? More cold air tingled his lungs.

"Keep breathing, you're doing great," Kate said again.

"I'm okay." He moved slowly, trying to stand. "I'm okay."

Kate was at his shoulder, one hand resting there, ready to grab him should he fall again. Airmed cupped his face in her hands, the same tingling feeling tickling his face.

Airmed wiped her thumb across Rafe's cheek, coming away with a slight wet sheen to it. Rubbing her finger and thumb together, Airmed had a curious look about her before she walked over to a shelf and took down a tall thin cylinder. She then reached into a bush that was growing on the wall, its leaves thick and sturdy, from within, she drew a small bottle of red liquid. She poured a small amount into the cylinder and then, squeezing her fingers together, caused a drop to fall into the glass. She swirled it, and then grabbed a lid which was pushed forcefully onto the cylinder.

"This here is very valuable," Airmed declared, holding the glass cylinder in front. "In all of time I can count on my hands the number of times someone has been given this. Remind me, Rafe, what is her name, the person you wish to save?"

"Evie." Rafe croaked out.

"Well, she is very lucky to have you. I don't give this to you lightly, and while you will never have another from me, I do like to know what becomes of those that I have helped. Therefore, when the time comes for Evie to pass, I wish to know what has become with her life from the extra time she was given." Airmed took a step closer towards Rafe, sending his heart pounding.

"I understand," Rafe said aloud while staring at the cylinder.

"Make sure you do." Airmed walked to the door. "Come, you have stayed here long enough. The god that live in this wood like their peace, myself included."

Airmed held out her hand with the cylinder. Rafe took the handful of strides in two bounds and clenched the glass in his hands, where the dark contents swirled inside.

This was it! He finally had it! Rafe gently placing it in his pocket next to the other vial. "Thank you. Thank you. You have no idea how much this means to me."

"Goodbye," Airmed said giving a rare smile, with her palm open towards the doorway. Kate strode through first, followed by Rafe.

"Rafe couldn't help but blink several times, taking in the green of the forest, even the air around them seemed to have a green tinge.

Kate was now on a path waving him over.

Rafe joined her, making their way along the path. He cast an eye behind to get one last view of Airmed. The mysterious and little-known goddess that had become the most important deity to Rafe, he swore he would worship her for all eternity.

He stood for a few seconds watching, knowing if she was there, she was hidden amongst her home of nature.

Rafe made his way along the path, following in Kate's footsteps, and feeling the weight of importance of what he carried in his pocket.

Chapter Fourteen

The gardens were eerily deserted this time when they walked through. Not even a glimpse of some wing or clothing.

"Where is everyone?" Rafe noticed Kate was fidgeting.

"I don't know," Kate said, her pace quickening as she played with the flap of her trouser pocket.

They emerged at the base of the hill to HOG and began to climb.

Kate stopped on the path in front. "Do you smell that?" Kate took in an extra deep breath.

Now that she mentioned it, there was a slight tinge of something wafting in the wind.

Kate took off at a jog and was at the top before Rafe. By the time he reached her, he was panting, lungs burning.

Standing next to Kate, he saw the source of the smell. Down the hill from HOG that led down to where the other buildings were, a small grey cloud of smoke floated, not quite able to crest the hill upon which they stood.

"What is that?" Rafe spoke aloud. More to himself than anything, nevertheless Kate still answered.

"Some sort of explosion."

She took off again, this time at a quicker pace. Rafe lengthened his strides to keep up but everything just bounced about and his joints ached with the constant pounding underfoot.

Oh gosh his lungs burned.

Rafe rounded a corner on the path down from HOG where he saw Kate with her hands on her head and shaking ever so slightly.

Now they were below the cloud of smoke, he was able to follow where she was staring. His eyes were drawn to a familiar building below. It had a number of steps leading up to it, however the roof was now in pieces and pockets of people were running away in various directions.

"What building is that?" Rafe said, even though he knew the answer.

Kate didn't answer, she just muttered to herself.

"Kate?"

"Yeah, what?" Kate snapped.

"The building, what is it?" Rafe asked again.

"This is not good, it's The Silent Chamber."

"The Silent Chamber?" Rafe repeated, his suspicions confirmed.

"Yes, the one I told you about before, where there are always seven angels guarding a portal. Nothing can leave or enter the portal unless you have the necessary knowledge of where you need to go. It's where all the secrets and treasures of HOG are kept. It's the safest place in this world, so if someone has breached it... then nowhere is safe."

"Should we go and check it out?" Rate suggested.

Kate stood there staring across the buildings and smoke rising up.

Patting the familiar shape in his breast pocket, Rafe walked down the hill in the direction of The Silent Chamber, leaving Kate in his wake. He now had two god' blood in his pocket and they needed to be used, so the sooner this incident was investigated the sooner he could save Evie.

He hadn't been watching where he'd been running as he mulled things over in his head, when he nearly tripped over. Holding his hands out to break his fall, he skidded on the loose pebbles.

"Ah!" Rafe cried out.

"The vials," Kate called out.

Rafe quickly stood and felt inside his jacket, taking out both, thankfully both were still intact.

"That's a relief," said Kate, as she passed him and continued down the path ahead.

As they jogged down the path, Kate kept egging him on. "Come on, quicker."

After being cajoled on the fourth time, Rafe instructed her to go ahead without him

"Are you sure?" Kate called back over her shoulder.

"I... am sure." He was so unfit, he was out of breath and getting fed up with always being the one left behind. Fed up with being slow. "Just go!" Rafe said waving her away.

Kate sprinted on ahead.

Following where he thought the Silent Chamber was located, Rafe made his way down the slight gradient. The streets were mostly empty with only a few figures darting around seeking cover. When he entered the open area in front of The Silent Chamber, a small crowd had gathered. Within were angels and god, discernible from some having wings and others having a lofty look about themselves.

Moving around a group of angels that had strange markings on their faces, he made his way to the steps, hoping to catch a glimpse of Kate.

Finally, he spied her, at the base of the stairs talking to a cloaked figure, whose dark robes which were probably once black but faded to a dark grey from the dust. At their feet lay a lifeless figure. What instantly struck Rafe, were the clawed hands that protruded from the sleeve of the garments.

Kate bent down to have a private word with the standing robed figure. Once they were finished, she spied Rafe and waved him over.

"So," Rafe said panting as he drew up to Kate, "what happened?"

"It seems someone exploded a bomb in The Silent Chamber killing the seven guards in the chamber itself and destroying large parts of the rest of the building." Kate indicating the prone figure on the floor. "This one tried to stop the intruder as they came out of the portal but they were too strong and were stabbed."

"Will it be okay?" Rafe asked bending down to take a closer look.

"Rafe, don't, they are very private," Kate said resting a hand on his shoulder. "It's already dead, I am afraid."

Rafe stood. "Came out of the portal? But I thought you said no one could enter or leave."

"They can't, not without knowing the necessary information," Kate said, her arms outstretched.

"But... But." Rafe tried to find the right words.

"I know, Rafe. But it just happened and no one knows how. That's not all either."

"What?"

"When they tried to stop the intruder, they noticed that he carried an item in his hand that was square shaped. They tried to follow but he was just too quick, but it sounds like..."

"Sebastian?" Rafe interjected.

"The description fits him," Kate said. "This is so bad Rafe I can't tell you." Placing her hands on her head. "This has never happened before and if he can break into the most secure place in HOG, then... nowhere is safe. We need to contact The Fates," Kate continued.

"Kate, I can't go with you."

"What?" Kate spun facing him.

"You seem to have this under control, and Sebastian is long gone. I need to go," Rafe said not making eye contact with Kate.

"Go. Go where?" Kate raised her voice.

"To see Evie. Now that I have a cure, I can bring her back." Rafe raised his head defiantly.

"Can't it wait? It's not as if she is going anywhere," Kate said but instantly scrunching her face up, almost as though she regretted blurting it out.

Rafe stood open mouthed.

Kate raised her hands in surrender. "I'm sorry, I shouldn't have said that. It was unkind of me, and I know you need to help your friend," Kate said.

"I have to go," Rafe said a little curtly. He thrust his hands forwards to open a portal at which, he heard a united inward intake of breath from around them. Before he stepped through, he saw the shocked faces of the crowd. To hell with them and this world, he thought, stepping through and not looking back.

On the other side, he found himself back in his room, staring at the clock which told him it was late at night. He pondered the idea of using a portal to travel to a more appropriate time, he was tired and wanted to just lay down for a moment before seeing Evie. Still in his clothes, he curled up on top of his duvet. And without realising or wanting it, the shroud of tiredness enveloped him.

Chapter Fifteen

What was that? Rafe's brain turbo charged from the noise that disturbed him.

"It's me," a voice called out.

Just his mum then.

Rafe rolled over to see what time it was. "Wow," Rafe said inadvertently at realising he has slept all night by mistake. It was still dark, although the light greys of dawn were appearing through a crack in his curtains.

"Your dad is going to drive you to school today as I have to pop into work early," his mum said, her head still peering around the door seemingly floating in mid-air.

"Okay, Mum," Rafe called as he stretched on his bed to get his joints moving.

"Did you sleep in your clothes again last night?" his mum queried.

Looking down at himself, he'd forgotten he was still in his clothes. "I guess so, I didn't realise how tired I was." He laid back and hitting the pillow hard with the back of his head.

"You have seemed a bit tired recently, perhaps the long sleep will have done you good."

He imagined the frown of concern across her face.

"Thanks, Mum. Have a good day at work." Rafe said trying to metaphorically close the door on this conversation

"Love you, Rafe," his mum said.

"Love you too, Mum."

With that, she left, leaving the door slightly ajar. Her way of letting him know that the world was waiting for him. Although he didn't want to go to school and wanted to see Evie, now that his mum had seen him, he couldn't bunk off and go visit her through a portal. He'd have to go along with it all, until school finished and he could get to Evie.

Rafe got changed and freshened himself up before he went downstairs.

His dad sat with Kira at the breakfast table and like clockwork, he had a coffee in hand. He wasn't quite sure what his dad did, it involved selling something and his head was always in a computer. When work finished though, he was always there for him.

"Hey, buddy." His dad had these names for him which were probably cute when he was little, but now that he was a teenager, they're probably less cute and more a way of his dad trying to relive Rafe's youth.

"Hey Dad," Rafe greeted him with a lopsided smile, trying to cover up how he really felt.

"It's going to be a good day today, I can feel it," his dad said as chirpy as ever.

"I have a lot on my mind, so I kind of just want to get school over with today."

His dad frowned at him. "Do you want to share what's on your mind?"

"No, it's okay."

"Seriously, I'm a pretty good listener, and you can try me out if you want?" Rafe's dad persisted.

"I'm okay. Seriously, I am, Dad, but thanks for the offer though." Rafe searched around for something to change the conversation to.

Rafe spied some food and grabbed a piece of toast, then slathered peanut butter on it. Mouth wide open, he stared at the mountain of peanut butter topping his food. What was he doing?

Taking a knife, he scraped half the thickness off and placed it back into the jar.

"Hey," Kira berated, "you're getting crumbs in the jar."

Ignoring his sister, Rafe took a bite. It tasted a bit bland but he knew he would feel less bloated from it.

After they had all eaten. Rafe sat in the back of the car, Kira always sat up front, she claimed it was elder sibling prerogative.

They arrived at school, Rafe entered the school grounds and hoped the day went without incident.

At the end of school, Rafe stood outside the school gates and waited for his sister to appear.

It didn't take him long before she rounded the corner with a friend in toe, who had long blonde hair in the neatest plait he had ever seen.

Rafe walked towards them.

"Kira," Rafe called out.

Both girls spun and, seeing who it was, they both scowled.

"What do you want?" Kira retorted with obvious disdain.

"I'm not going to get a ride with Dad today, will you tell him?" Rafe said.

"He's not going to like that." Kira said while swatting away some flying bug next to her. "Where are you going anyway?"

"I'm going to the hospital," Rafe said slowly.

Kira's face softened a little. "Ah. To see your friend."

"Yeah." Rafe eyed the ground, not wanting to make eye contact.

"I'll tell him, don't worry," Kira said with her chin held up high.

"Thanks," Rafe said and he meant it. Kira had been supportive of his visiting and caring for Evie ever since she had been in hospital.

"And Rafe?" Kira added.

"Yes."

"I hope she gets better soon." Evie and her immaculately haired friend stalked off, their hair swinging side to side in their bobbles.

Rafe made his way through a different school gate and walked in the direction of the hospital. All day he'd waited to get to Evie, placing his hand on his breast to make sure the familiar vial was there.

Walking the streets of his hometown gave him time to reflect on the past few days. He knew he should care about what happened in HOG and above all, it made him feel like he was important in life, that he belonged to something, although at this moment, he couldn't care less. None of it mattered while Evie was still on the edge of life. He got her into this mess, and he was determined to get her out.

After thirty minutes of walking, his feet were sore, and he was relieved to pass through the automatic doors of the hospital.

Getting in the lift to the necessary floor, he pressed the worn and faded button. When it opened onto the correct floor, his feet took him down the strobe lit corridor which he had walked too many times to count. He passed the same room which he had overheard the doctor speaking to Evie's mum, giving her the news that she might be moved.

Turning into Evie's room, he saw the familiar cards, flowers and teddies that adorned the room. And, as usual, in the bed was Evie in the same position he had left her the last time. He knew underneath the tranquillity though, a constant battle ensued. Her body fighting against the hidden poison from the wound created by a magic knife.

With a sigh, he made his way around the bed to the other side so that he faced the door rather than backed onto it.

Reaching into his pocket, he took out the two vials. One simple and rounded from Prometheus, while the other was shaped with ridges from Airmed. One for him and one for Evie.

Airmed had said that if one were to be drunk in its entirety, then it would leave a long-standing imprint in their blood of the magic it contained.

Taking the smooth shaped vial, he undid the stopper, placed it against his lips and lifted. It took three gulps which made him gag and nearly vomit. Swallowing three large mouthfuls was a lot different to swallowing a single drop from a fingertip, and now that he had done it, he didn't feel any different if truth were told.

Now that he was here though, he realised he hadn't thought about how to get the liquid into Evie's system. He walked over to a disposable paper towel dispenser on the wall and took a piece, folding it over and then carefully placed it under Evie's chin. Her lips were slightly apart so, using a few fingers, Rafe wiggled her jaw open.

Delving into his pocket for the vial that Airmed gave him, he withdrew it from his pocket. But before he could take the lid off, footsteps echoed down the corridor.

Rafe took his hand off Evie and stuffed the paper towel into his pocket.

The door opened and in came Evie's mum. Rafe's heart pounded, that had been close.

"Oh. Hi. I wasn't expecting anyone else here," she said. "You're Evie's friend, aren't you? I've seen you in here coming and going. I'm Jean by the way, Evie's mum."

"Hi," Rafe tried to say but came out in a croak. "Did you want me to leave?" Rafe asked, hoping she would say no.

"Oh, that's kind of you, dear, but I just popped back in to say goodbye. I was speaking to the doctor in her office."

Rafe didn't say anything to that, what could he say after all?

"I've seen you come and go before. What's your name?"

"I'm Rafe, I'm one of Evie's friends."

"Well, it's nice to meet you, Rafe. How do you know her?"

"We go to school together," Rafe said simply.

"That's nice, I didn't realise she was close to a boy at school." Jean placed her hand on her chest.

Rafe felt himself go red, and his neck started to itch.

Jean approached the bed where her daughter lay and again tried to strike up a conversation. "I just mean, she never really spoke of friends at school before."

"To be honest, we never really spoke much at school. We only became friends recently outside of school during the summer." He picked his words carefully making sure he didn't reveal his presence during her stabbing. "But we became close, and she's now one of my best friends."

Jean smiled, which to Rafe seemed tinged with a little sadness. He saw her bottom lip wobble. "No one knows how she ended up here you know?"

Rafe did know that. The Fates had ensured no one remembered them bringing her in.

"She'll be okay, I know it," Rafe tried to reassure her.

"I hope you're right. They want to move her to somewhere more suitable for her needs."

Rafe unconsciously plunged his hand in his pocket for the familiar feel of Airmed's vial.

Jean must have realised his anxiousness, as she tried to soothe him. "It's okay, my dear, she will be well cared for. It's only across town, so she'll be moved in the next few days once they've organised transportation and finalised her paperwork. Perhaps you can still visit there?" Jean's eyebrows raised, almost pleading.

"Of course." Rafe knew he would have visited even if he wasn't asked.

Jean leant forwards to give Evie a kiss, her hair, the same dark colour, draped over Evie. Jean whispered something in Evie's ear, and Rafe saw a tear well up in her eye. Rafe watched it as it gently glided down her cheek and thought it would fall onto Evie's peaceful face, until Jean stood at the last moment and wiped her face.

"I miss her, you know."

"I know," is all Rafe could say. "Me too."

With a heavy sigh, she waved her goodbye. "It was nice to meet you, and I hope to see you again. Take care." Then she was gone.

Rafe played with his hands, fingers interlocked in a tight embrace. He hadn't noticed when he started pacing the room. On one circuit, Rafe jolted to a stop as a nurse appeared at the doorway. She had dark hair tied in a pony tail and a simple face touched by only a little makeup. She wore thick ridged glasses that made her eyes look large through the lens.

"Hi there, don't mind me, I'm just doing a set of observations on her," the nurse said.

"Oh, would you like me to go?" Rafe offered.

"In a moment, as we need to change her wounds."

The nurse placed her fingers on Evie's wrist, the other eyeing a watch appended to her nurse's uniform. After a minute had passed by in silence, she placed something on her finger, a series of numbers flashed until it settled on the number ninety-nine.

The nurse moved over to the computer and tapped in a series of numbers and letters.

"Right, that's me done."

"Nurse?" Rafe asked.

"Yes."

"Sorry to bother you. I wanted to ask about Evie if that's okay?" Rafe tailed off at the end.

"Of course."

Rafe was always astounded by a nurse's patience, the ones he had met had always had time to speak to him even though they undoubtedly had a million things to do.

"Her mum mentioned that Evie was going to be moved to another hospital."

"Yes, she is to go across town. They have a ward for long term cases that are high dependency. Evie is okay, we're just waiting for her wound to heal. Which is proving quite tricky. But we need the room, as a lot of people come and go through this hospital. She'll be well cared for there and can stay for as long as she needs to."

"When will she be moved?"

"All being well," the nurse said. "Hopefully tomorrow afternoon."

As Rafe didn't have anything else to say, the nurse took this for a sign that the conversation had ended and began to move towards the door. "I'll just grab some more bandages from the draw next door, and then I'll have to ask you to vacate the room."

"Thank you, nurse," Rafe called out.

"You're welcome." And with that she left.

So, he had until tomorrow then.

Rafe was reluctantly making his way back home on foot having not completed his objective of curing Evie.

Walking the streets home, he felt an unnerving presence somewhere. Glancing back, even though he couldn't see anyone, the hairs on his arms stood on end. Wrapping his jacket around him, he quickened his pace.

Taking a look in either direction, he crossed the road, passing just behind a car that drove past.

Rafe still felt the lingering sense of someone following him, and once he was on the other side of the road, he twisted to see who it was.

Standing not ten metres away was the person following him with her familiar wavy brown hair. Kate's face was the same as before, but perhaps a little less sad.

"You scared the living daylights out of me. What are you doing here?" Rafe panted holding his chest.

"We need you," Kate said flatly.

"You need me?" Rafe searched around to make sure they were not drawing unwanted attention.

"Yes," Kate said.

"Why? What's happened?"

"I'm hearing of some worrying things about Jupiter and his allies," Kate said more sternly than before, which worried Rafe. "He's threatening to bring down HOG and the triumvirate for starters. Something is wrong, this isn't usual behaviour for a god."

"What do you want me to do? You have all the other Grey Guardians," Rafe asked.

"We're pushed to the limit, we're at breaking point, and you are closer to this than any of them."

"Not as much as you," Rafe retorted back, but instantly regretted it when Kate winced. To Rafe's relief, Kate was gracious enough to let it slide.

"You know Sebastian, you know what we're looking for. He also likes you.` I can tell," Kate said with an eyebrow raised.

"Although he threw some sort of enchanted knife at us?" Rafe felt his voice raise a notch.

"One day we'll find out why he did that, but at this very moment, I'm the leader of the Grey Guardians, and I can't do this without you. I need you," Kate said which raised hairs along Rafe's back. It was the first time he had heard anyone say they needed him.

Rafe straightened his back. "What can we do to stop Jupiter, we're not exactly god ourselves?"

Kate stepped forward and grabbed his elbow, directing him in the direction of his home. "We should continue to walk as we talk, in case anyone is listening." As they made their way down the street, Kate continued. "You're right, we can't stop them physically, so we need to find evidence of what is going on to show everyone. Maybe then, cooler heads will prevail."

"Why don't we just tell everyone what we know already?" Rafe suggested.

"We need tangible proof beyond doubt. Everyone's tempers have boiled over, and they won't listen to reason, they need tangible proof that is beyond reproach. If we don't stop this, then all of HOG will be dragged into this conflict and remember; what happens in HOG affects us mortals down here." Kate pulled Rafe out of the way of a pedestrian.

Kate might be right, but his mind was set on only one thing. Evie. His mind could not focus on anything, and his body was consumed by anxiety which made him feel sick. They walked for some time in silence until Rafe couldn't take it anymore.

"I haven't healed Evie yet," Rafe said.

"What? Why not?" Kate spluttered.

Rafe spotted that they were nearly at his house.

"I was going to give her some of Airmed's blood, then her mum came in and then a nurse, so I ran out of time."

"She isn't going anywhere. Can't it wait?" Kate said almost pleadingly.

"No, it can't. It's all I think about at the moment, and I can't focus on anything else."

"Ok!" Kate holding her hands up. "Okay, I get it. I suppose the longer you keep hold of the vial, the easier it could get lost, stolen or broken as well."

Rafe hadn't thought about that, but now that he was made aware of it, it was even more essential that he got it inside of her.

They rounded a corner and were now on Rafe's street. "This is me," he said letting Kate know he could go on by himself.

"Great, let's go then." Kate stepped ahead of Rafe.

"Wha... where are you going?" Trying to keep up, she stormed ahead.

"Which one is it? Is it the one with a green door?"

"No, it's the one with a grey door," Rafe said with a little trepidation.

"That's ironic, don't you find?" Kate flashed a smile as she moved towards the grey door.

"Are you coming in?" Rafe stumbled after her and nearly clattered into the back of Kate. He held out his arms to grab something as he skidded on the loose chippings of the road. There were patches of wet black asphalt dotted across his street, from when the local authorities didn't tarmac their street properly the year before

"Of course, I am coming with you. Listen, I need you and if you aren't coming until you have got that... stuff into Evie. Then I am going to help you, the sooner I can get you back to HOG to help me, the better."

"Okay. Okay." Rafe held his palms up. "I'm sure my parents can add a place for you at the table."

Rafe opened the house with his key and stepped into the hallway. He popped his head around the lounge door to find no one there. Then he walked into the kitchen, which was not so empty. Rafe was about to back up when Kate pushed him forward, forcing him to stumble into the door and push it open.

Kira and her two girlfriends turned in unison at the intrusion.

"Arghh!" Rafe yelled, grabbing hold of the breakfast bar to steady himself. Kira and her friends stared open mouthed, with a box of pizza in front of them. "Sorry, I lost my footing there. Where's Mum and Dad?" Rafe said as he stared at the pizza box and avoided the eyes of the two girls, whom Rafe recognised from school. They were part of the popular group of which Kira belonged, one was tall, with dark straight hair. While the other had short blonde hair, in a pixie style. Although different, they were both very pretty.

"They were called out to an emergency." Kira held up a note that had writing and numbers on it.

"What sort of emergency?"

"Uncle Stephen and Auntie Alex were in an accident. Bizarre really, they were walking on the pavement and were hit by a car. They're okay, just banged up. Dad's gone to hospital to see how they are, while Mum has gone to their house to look after our cousins." Rafe thought of his two young cousins, Poppy and Lily, who were much younger than him and would be scared now.

"Hi, by the way." Kira raised a hand and waved towards Kate.

"Hi," Kate replied nonchalantly.

Rafe kept switching his gaze between Kira and Kate, wondering what his sister thought. While Kira and Kate were similar in age, Kate looked older than all of them. Grizzled from years as a Grey Guardian, she carried herself in such a manner, which may as well have been a sign that said '*danger keep out of my way*'.

"Rafe, are you not going to introduce us?" Kira said curtly.

"Err, yes. This is Kate, a friend of mine." Rafe noticed the long dark-haired friend raised her eyebrows. "Kate, this is my sister Kira and her friends."

"Nice to meet you," Kira said in an unusually friendly way, which clearly meant she wanted more information.

"Likewise. Shall we go upstairs to talk, Rafe?" Kate nodded towards the stairs.

"Erm, yes."

Kate made her way to the stairs.

"One second, Kira, do you have any spare pizza?"

"Dad ordered two boxes before he left. There's a spare next to the fridge for you."

Rafe pondered if his sister would have volunteered the food before he went upstairs if she hadn't been asked directly for it. He opened the lid to a wall of smell that made his mouth water. His dad had picked well by ordering a vegetarian pizza. Rafe preferred them over a meat one as he just thought the meat on pizzas tasted a bit too fake. He grabbed the box and headed upstairs.

Kira yelled at his back. "Mum and Dad don't think they will be back tonight. So, we're going to watch a movie later and then have a sleepover. Okay?"

"Yeah. Yeah," Rafe said to himself not bothering to turn around and answer. As he went up the stairs, he heard one of Kira's friends speaking in a hushed tone. "Did you see how old she was?"

Another voice joined in. "I know. You don't think they are... dating do you?"

"Ewwww," Rafe heard his sister's disgusted voice.

He couldn't be bothered to eavesdrop anymore and rounded the banister on the landing, to see Kate waiting there.

"Nice sister," Kate commented as her arms folded across her chest.

Rafe didn't know what to add to that. He guessed that at some level Kira must love him, but then they weren't all that close anymore, not since they were young.

"This is my room." Rafe pushed a door open and to his relief saw his bed made up, although he had left a load of dirty washing on the floor. Rafe ran in and threw the pizza box onto the bed, then scooped the dirty clothes up and placed them in his laundry bin. When he finished, he surveyed his handiwork and spied Kate in the corner of his eye, leaning against the door frame, arms crossed and one eyebrow cocked.

"You sure know how to impress a girl."

Rafe spluttered, "Erm. I. Ah," unable to get his words out.

"Easy, soldier." Kate walked towards a small bookcase. "You're not my type."

Rafe had never assumed he was, but her playfulness really caught him off guard.

Once Kate had stopped fingering his volume of books, she walked over to his bed and opened up the pizza box.

The smell drifted over to Rafe.

Kate grabbed a piece and took a bite, prompting Rafe to take a place opposite Kate and take a piece of pizza as well.

"See anything you like on my shelf?" Rafe asked with his mouth full of food.

"One of two." Kate swallowed what was in her mouth. "I like looking at book shelves." She took another slice of pizza. "You can tell a lot about someone by the choice of their books."

That was an interesting thought. "How so?" Rafe wolfed down a slice and reached for another.

"People generally only keep the books that mean something to them. Most people either read a book and give it away or read digital books, so they only keep or buy physical copies if it has a deep connection to them. Your books, for instance, say to me that you want to escape reality, that you want to live a different life and be the hero for once."

She was right, of course, Rafe thought, and it was all over his bookshelf when you came to think of it. He'd obviously been quiet longer than normal as Kate reached over and placed a hand on his knee.

"Hey, I didn't mean to upset you, I just say what I see. And don't even think to ask what my books say about me." She gave a wink.

Kate grabbed another slice which tempted Rafe, but he held back for once.

"Why?" Although he could guess what her bookshelf was like, given her obsession with Sebastian. "Afraid people might actually know you're nice deep down?"

"Ouch." Kate wiped her mouth with the back of her hand.

A loud cheer came from downstairs, indicating that the party was cranking up a notch.

"So, let's get down to business," Kate suggested. "So in regards to Evie, what's the plan?"

"I give her a little of the blood, hope she revives enough for me to administer the whole lot?" Rafe sighed.

"If that doesn't work, then perhaps there's an artefact of some sort which can help?"

"What do you mean?" There was one slice of pizza left. Rafe's mouthed craved it but before he reached for it, he pushed his stomach out to feel how full it was. Realising he didn't need, it he pushed the box towards Kate.

"You sure?" Kate cocked an eyebrow.

"Yeah, I'm sure, I'm full anyway. So, what do you mean by artefacts?"

"Well, there are several artefacts and items that hold unique powers, perhaps there is one which could help us. The problem is that I don't specifically know of any which could help. Although, I'm just wondering if there is anyone we could ask." She threw herself back onto the bed, so that she laid backwards with her hands on her eyes, shutting out the world while she thought. "Think, Kate. Think."

After a few moments silence, Rafe couldn't stand it anymore. "Anything coming to mind?"

"Ah, nothing yet. We could ask a warlock perhaps."

"It's a start at least," Rafe mused. "Would a warlock know of a spell to transfer the blood into her?"

"Perhaps. I'll ask around in the shadow world. I'm planning on visiting some of the important shadow creatures over the coming days. Maybe Lithien will know."

"Who's that?" Rafe wondered at the strange name.

"She's a Faerie, I'm meant to be meeting her in a few days to convince her of siding with us. I worked with her alongside Sebastian a long time ago and she has a lot of influence amongst her kind. She may give us what we need for Evie, but at a price."

"A price?"

"Yes, you don't get to be influential amongst the Faeries without being cunning and getting what you want. If we leave now, we could go and meet her," Kate suggested.

Louder laughs came from downstairs.

"I would love nothing better than to meet a Faerie. But now that Kira knows I am here, if I were to disappear, she would tell my parents," Rafe said, he wasn't sure of why he wasn't keen on going, but something held him back.

"But we can arrive back at the same time, she would never know."

"True, but we can't go to the hospital tonight anyway, it's shut now, and we can't go forward in time as Kira would notice I wasn't here."

"What about if we return back in time?"

"It just doesn't feel right to me. It would in effect erase out everything that just happened over the last few hours."

"And?" Kate's arms were outstretched.

"I can't just keep going back in time to fix our problems. Sometimes we must let time continue and face what's ahead of us." Rafe surprised himself by what he had just said.

"Really? I'd never have thought you to be of the type. Anika is the same as you, she would never go back in time unless it was the only way. Personally, if I need to fix something I just go and fix it with no messing around."

Rafe just stared, noting how different she was from him.

"What?" Kate caught him staring. "I just don't like waiting around, that's all."

"Let's try my way first tomorrow, and if it doesn't work, we'll try yours. Okay?"

"Fair enough, so what shall we do in the meantime then?" Kate scanned the room.

Rafe saw his case on the floor and reached over. He delved inside, pulling out a laptop. "We can watch something while we wait?" Rafe suggested as he pressed the keys.

"Fine, but I'm choosing." Kate sidled up to Rafe.

After some flicking through, Kate settled on a Japanese black and white film with sub titles. A classic, she assured him.

Sitting on the bed, Rafe propped some pillows behind him as the laptop balanced on a side table in front of them. Both their knees bunched up to their chins.

As Rafe watched the film, he had to admit he was enjoying it, but after some time, he found his eyes grow heavy.

"Where's the loo?" Kate jumped off the bed, and Rafe's eyes shot open, realising he had almost fallen asleep.

"First door on the right," Rafe slurred.

Kate paused the film and with a rush of wind from the door flying open, she was gone.

He'd shut his eyes for a split second before he heard Kate return. "Right, let's get back to watching this movie." Kate pressed a button, starting the film again.

Rafe let the words flash across the screen, not noticing his eyes close.

Chapter Sixteen

Rafe woke on his bed curled up in a ball. As he stretched, he felt the rough feel of his clothes on him again. He had to stop sleeping in his clothes, he cussed himself. Surveying around him, he saw the laptop on top of the table placed back in the corner but Kate was nowhere to be seen.

Rafe got up, picked up a pair of clean boxer shorts from his drawer and ambled over to the shower room. Once he was suitably clean, he got out, dried himself quickly and put his clean boxer shorts on. Wrapping the towel around him, he bunched up the dirty washing into his arms and made his way back to his room. He pushed the door open and nearly dropped them and the towel when he saw Kate sitting cross legged on his bed.

"What are you doing here! You scared me." Rafe placed the pile on his laundry bin.

Kate smirked, eyeing him up. Rafe suddenly felt very exposed with his belly hanging out, so he opened a drawer and put on a polo shirt. Then he found some clean jeans and put them on under his towel.

"Well, Rafe," Kate said in a lofty voice, "you do know how to impress a girl." He knew she was trying to make a joke but also knew he was no picture. Unbeknown to Kate, her comment stung him.

"How did you get in? Where did you go?" Rafe steered her down a different conversation.

"I fell asleep like you, then when I woke up, I transitioned back home, washed and put on some new clothes for the day ahead." She held out a cup of something hot. Rafe wrinkled his nose and peered at it. He didn't usually drink hot drinks, but he took it anyway. "I saw your sister downstairs by the way," Kate continued. "It's safe to say she was surprised that I was still here and probably thinks I stayed with you."

Rafe felt his ears redden.

"Don't sweat it, Rafe. Let her think what she wants, it can't hurt your reputation anyway."

Is that what he really wanted? He didn't think of Kate that way though.

Rafe took a sip of his drink, thinking of anything to get past this conversation. "Right, let's get started then!"

Entering the hospital room, Evie lay there unmoving as she has done for weeks. Approaching the bed, Rafe took out the bottle.

"I'll keep an eye on the corridor," Kate said as she leaned against the door frame.

Rafe felt more comfortable this time as he extracted Airmed's bottle. Pulling the stopper off, he placed his thumb over the top and turned it upside down. Once he had placed it back upright, on his thumb was a small pool of red liquid. Rafe opened Evie's mouth and squeezed a few drops within. He was excited and apprehensive all in one go.

Grabbing the paper towel, he wiped his thumb, replaced the stopper on the bottle and carefully placed it back in his pocket.

Kate meandered to the bed, now that Rafe had finished, and she stroked Evie's face tenderly.

"Blood never taste's nice no matter what," Kate said in a slow voice.

A memory which seemed long ago came to Rafe, of saying ritual words, which now seemed silly, then drinking something that tasted... metallic.

"It was blood in the cup, wasn't it? When we take our oath as Grey Guardians," Rafe said but hoping the answer was negative.

"Yes. It's The Fates' blood, all three of theirs mixed. They have the power to go through the timeline, so by drinking their blood we permanently gain their power to do so as well."

A beeping noise began to chime, breaking their bubble. Rafe searched around for it and walked over to a monitor that showed waving lines and numbers.

What had they done, Rafe thought.

Rafe and Kate sat outside on some seats, fake leather stretched over metal to give the illusion of comfort, but they were far from it. Rafe eyed the clock on the wall. The last ten minutes had seemed like an hour as the nurses and doctors walked back and forth from the room.

Rafe went over in his head the sequence of events that had led him to this point. When they had been at the beeping machine, three nurses stormed in and while one of them ushered Kate and himself out, two others busied themselves at the machine and Evie.

He clamped his hands together, his fingers interlaced on his lap, the whites of his knuckles and fingers palpable. What had they done?

"Excuse me?" someone called out.

Rafe raised his head to find a nurse standing in the doorway. "Yes?"

"Evie has started to come around."

Finally, he could breathe, not realising he had been holding his breath.

"She's still very weak, and we're going to restrict guests to family only, to enable her to recover her strength quicker. Are you her boyfriend or family?"

Rafe's mouth formed shapes, however no words came out.

"Yes, he is." Rafe heard next to him. He shot a look sideways at Kate who continued to speak. "He's just in a little shock, I'll wait here, Rafe." Kate nodded towards the door.

Rafe tentatively stood up, rubbing his sweaty hands along his trousers. Then he shuffled towards the doorway.

In the room, propped up on the pillow and eyes shut, was Evie. He approached the bed, and careful not to disturb any of the wires she was connected to, he cocked his head to the side to see if there was a gap under her eyelids.

"I know you're there," she whispered hoarsely.

The nurse still stood there. "Her throat is sore from not using it for so long. I'll leave you for a couple of minutes, and then I'll have to ask you to leave."

After the nurse left, Rafe saw the corners of Evie's mouth curl up. "I didn't realise I had a boyfriend."

Rafe felt butterflies doing somersaults in his stomach. He was so happy she was back, smiling from ear to ear.

"Ah, you weren't meant to hear that. Kate was just trying to get me in to see you."

"Kate?" Evie asked, licking her cracked lips.

"Another Grey Guardian. I have so much to tell you, Evie, but the only way you'll be properly healed is if you drink this vial of blood." Rafe held the red swirling liquid in his hand.

"Ugh." Evie croaked.

"I found a god who has the power to heal and bring people back from the dead, so I squeezed a few drops into your mouth and... here you are." Rafe waved his hands at Evie laying in the bed. "Your wound is cursed though. It doesn't want to knit itself back together permanently, so I don't know how long the few drops we gave you will last for."

Rafe spotted on a side table a polystyrene cup with a red and white straw. He snatched the straw up and placed it in the vial.

"Do... I... have to?" Evie sounded weaker.

"I don't know how much time you have. I'm sorry, please take a sip," Rafe pleaded.

Placing it between her lips, Rafe saw the shadow of liquid rise within. She took one gulp, then another, draining half the vial.

"I'm... sleep..."

Rafe gently shook her and placed the straw between her lips again. "Please, just a little more." Rafe gave another gentle shake, and the shadow of liquid rose again. "Just a little more, nearly there." Rafe encouraged until nothing was left inside the bottle.

He heard footsteps down the corridor, so quickly took some paper and wiped her mouth.

Squeezing her hand, he murmured his goodbye. "I'll be back. I promise."

He hesitated forwards with his head, thought better of it and took a step back. An impulse took hold, and he stepped forwards, gently placing his lips on her forehead.

"Okay, it's time now." The same nurse was at the door. "You seem smiley." The nurse smirked.

Outside the room, Kate was waiting. "So?"

Rafe indicated the corridor, and they walked towards the stairs.

"She drank it!" Rafe couldn't hold in his excitement anymore and ran his hand through his hair. "I'm so relieved that it worked, Kate!"

"I'm pleased for you, Rafe. We're Grey Guardians, and we stick together. We may be small in number, but together we can accomplish anything." They rounded a corner and next to a lamppost was a coffee cart.

"Welcome ta the greatest coffee car' around. We 'ave the world's finest groun' beans!" said a familiar voice

"Yeah right." Rafe smiled to himself.

Nearing the cart, a slouching figure tossed food around. Rafe chuckled slightly when Kate jumped in surprise.

"Ah look at you two," Sherlock's thick accent called out. "Nice ta see ya still workin' together." He lowered his voice to a whisper. "I 'eard who's back in town. I always liked that Sebastian as well but it jus' goes ta show, ya never can tell about someone."

Rafe could almost feel Kate stiffen.

"So why are you here, Sherlock?" Rafe probed.

"I 'ave been sent 'ere by management, ya see. Ya both are needed desperately in HOG. War 'as broken out and sides taken."

"Who's started the war?" Kate said with a touch of panic to her voice.

"Jupiter's lot, they 'ave gone crazy. Accusing everyone an' anyone."

"What can we do?" Rafe also felt worried.

"Not sure, but all Grey Guardians 'ave been given new assignments. You are ta go ta the Silent Chamber an' find out wha' happened there." Sherlock grabbed both hands of his cart and lifted. "Tis 'as been a quiet day 'ere, I think I'll find better pastures."

They watched as Sherlock rounded a corner, pushing his cart slowly in front.

There was something about Sherlock that always confounded Rafe. "Why does Sherlock always have food or drink to sell? Why doesn't he ever just come up to you and tell you the message?"

"When you figure it out, let the rest of us know, will you, we've been wondering the same thing as well," Kate answered.

"Are you okay about what he said?" Rafe didn't have to specify what he meant

Kate shrugged her shoulder. "What can be done about it, Sebastian is what he is."

Rafe pondered this for a moment, not sure what she meant. Rafe knew from Alesia that she was more upset about him than she let on but pressing her would help no one.

"So, to the Silent Chamber then," Rafe suggested.

Kate led them down a secluded side alley where she thrust forwards with her hands and opened a gap, which they both stepped through

Chapter Seventeen

A thick haze of smoke encompassed HOG whichever way Rafe looked. A scent of fire clung in the air and to either side, buildings were knocked through. Black smouldering scorch marks pocketed any wall left standing. In front were the steps to the Silent Chamber with the door off its hinges.

The last time he had seen it, it was smouldering with a mushroom of smoke coming from atop. Now the place was deserted, the hustle and bustle of the place from before gone.

“I'm surprised it hasn't been repaired yet,” Rafe pondered aloud.

Kate raised her eyebrows. “And why is that?”

“Well, they're god, they should be able to fix anything with a flick of a finger.” Rafe kicked a pebble along the floor.

“It doesn't work like that. Besides, the Silent Chamber isn't run by the god, it's run by a race from the shadow world.”

“Who?” Rafe asked, remembering a figure motionless on the floor, with a clawed hand peeking out of its sleeve.

"To be honest, I don't know what they are but you'll see them soon enough." Kate waved her arm towards the door.

Rafe said, "That doesn't fill me with confidence," as he followed her slowly, ensuring Kate was always one step ahead.

Standing before the great doors, Rafe cast a look behind them. The place was like something from a war movie and eerily quiet.

The door, which once must have been formidable, was now propped up against the wall.

Kate shrugged her shoulders at Rafe. "I guess we just knock." Kate pulled the still-intact door knocker and let it go with a clang.

Would anyone hear that? Rafe wondered. After no movement came from within the doorway, Rafe leant forward to attempt a louder knock.

Dark claws clamped around the edge of the frame and a hooded figure emerged from within.

"Keeper of the chamber." Kate stammered, clearly startled like Rafe was.

The figure stood without replying.

Kate cleared her throat. "We've come to search the Silent Chamber for clues of who did this." Opening her palms and arms out to indicate the rubble strewn square around them.

"We do not need your help." A quiet hiss came from the hooded figure.

The fact that it hissed in a whisper was the scariest part of all, but close behind was the *we* part. How many more of them were there?

"The person that broke into your chamber, stole something valuable, didn't they?"

The figure stood still.

"We know they did." Kate persevered, "they were after something and found a way to break in and out. I'm not the only one around here who can figure that out. But have you found out how they did it yet?"

Again, there was no answer.

"We can help you find how they did it, so you can ensure it doesn't happen again. Then to make things even better for you, we'll track down that person."

The figure still stood motionlessly. Rafe was about to open his mouth and say something, however he was relieved to be beaten to it.

"*We accept your proposal,*" their host said.

The door widened, and Kate stepped forwards.

Inside, wooden panelling layered the stonework, at least where the panelling hadn't been ripped apart by the force of the blast. Walking down a corridor that passed other rooms, each a scene of chaos from fallen debris. The roof was mostly intact but, in some places, it had fallen to allow shafts of light to light up the rooms.

Rafe had to step over several fallen pieces of stone, also noting a canvas picture among the debris, which Rafe thought was a peculiar object. In one of the rooms he passed, he spied two other cloaked figures deep in conversation.

They arrived in a wide chamber where a doorway shimmered in the middle of the room.

"What's that?" Rafe asked.

"It's a portal, to where, no one knows. Only the keepers of the chamber go into it, rumour has it that someone once attempted to sneak in, and they never came back. Supposedly there is a lot of security on the other side, which is why this portal is used by everyone to store their most precious of possessions," Kate said with her hands placed on her hips.

He was about to roll off his tongue, *until now* but thought better of it given the company, they were in. Their hooded guide walked over to another of their kind that stooped over a pile of rubble.

No words passed between them, or at least none that Rafe could discern. But the crouching figure stood up and turned its head in their direction.

"Did you see that?" Rafe said his mouth wide open.

"See what?" Kate was surveying the room, taking it all in.

"They communicated to each other, even though I heard no words." Rafe just couldn't believe what he had witnessed.

"No, I didn't. I suggest we just get the job done, and then get out of here, alright?" Kate suggested a little uneasily.

"Agreed." Rafe would have preferred to have avoided being here altogether, however he had had no choice in the matter.

Both hooded figures now strode over to them, and Rafe couldn't help but sway on his feet. Spying in the hand of the one who had been sifting through the rubble was a piece of twisted metal. What was it? Rafe squinted and craned his neck to try and see it better.

"What brings The Grey Guardians here?" hissed one of the approaching figures.

Although all the figures look identical with their matching clothes and hidden faces, Rafe had noticed a subtle difference in shade of cloak between these two hooded figures. The one that spoke to them and who had been sifting through the rubble had a cloak that was off black, as though faded with age. While his companion who had greeted them at the door had a darker shade of black, a newer cloak, mused Rafe.

Rafe just stared at Kate for a response as this was her gig anyway.

"The person that did this to you, we believe it is the same person we are after."

"*And what would they come here for*?" said the figure with the faded cloak.

"An item stored here long ago." Kate pointed towards the portal.

"Do you recognise this?" The hooded figure finally held out the piece of twisted metal.

Kate took it, she turned it side to side, and Rafe couldn't help himself as he also leaned over. The twisted metal was tall and had a wide base, and the patterns on it were familiar.

"Look." Kate nudged Rafe and fingered a familiar symbol with swirling lines.

"The Cup of Poseidon!" Rafe whispered.

"You're right!" Kate exclaimed. "This is the Cup of Poseidon," Kate said louder for all to hear. "Rafe took it from King Minos, who gave it to The Fates."

Rafe placed his hands on his hips, closed his eyes and tried connecting the loose ends. When he opened his eyes, Rafe still played with the item while the two hooded figures looked in his direction, unnerving him.

Rafe moved away and pretended to look through the rubble for clues while he tried to piece it all together. As he crouched down and absent-mindedly picked up a piece of masonry, he twizzled it in hands. Casting a glance towards Kate, she had a puzzled look about her as the two hooded figures stood waiting.

Rafe discarded the loose masonry and ambled over. "So, the cup was from King Minos."

"What was that?" Kate called out from across the room.

"Just re-treading my steps." Rafe said. "So, the cup was from King Minos, and we gave it to The Fates, and they must have put it into the portal. Can anyone go into the portal?"

"*Only we can enter the portal safely*," said one of the hooded figures, Rafe couldn't tell which.

"I... err. Don't mean to pry. But why is that?"

The two figures faced each other, and no words were spoken, but it seemed a silent permission was granted.

"*The portal enters a realm not of this world.*"

"Sebastian went through it and came back alive it seems," Rafe said a little smugly.

One of the figures cocked their head sideways, it would have seemed comical to Rafe if the situation wasn't so serious.

"Could Sebastian have put a tracking device on the cup? He had access to it in Ancient Greece," Rafe suggested.

"True," Kate answered. "He certainly had the means and opportunity, so why would he put a tracker on the cup. There's no way he could have known the cup would be put in the Silent Chamber, and that's where a part of the Book of Sorothir was evidently placed."

Rafe noted the shift in stance of one of the figures before them. Rafe glanced up to see it was the one with the faded hood.

"First, he would have to know it was in the portal, fight past the seven Angelic Guards, navigate through the portal, locate it and then get out," Kate suggested a little incredulously.

"Which he seemingly did." Rafe pointed out, waving both arms around to highlight his point. "I have to admit though, it is far-fetched."

Kate pursed her lips into a thin line. "He was incredible, and everyone gravitated towards him. When he was our leader, you knew you'd always come out on top, and he had the answers to everything." She cleared her throat. "I think it's time we left though, I don't think there is anything else to gain from sticking around. I'm ready when you are."

Outside, they took a walk down the road, making sure they were out of earshot.

"Did you see how one of them shifted when you mentioned the Book of Sorothir?" Rafe quizzed.

"Yes! Which means they knew they were in possession of part of the book. Something is up here." Kate rubbed her chin. "I can't put my finger on it. I think we need to report it to The Fates as soon as we can."

"Okay then, follow me." Rafe began to clasp his hands together.

"What are you doing? You can't just turn up to where The Fates live!" Kate rounded on Rafe.

"Why not? I have Prometheus' blood in me now remember, I can bypass any barrier." Rafe couldn't stop the corner of his mouth twitching.

"I forgot about that." Kate scratched her head. "They're going to hate it, now that you can drop in on them anytime." Kate threw her head back and barked a laugh. "Let's do it."

Rafe thrust his hands forward, tearing a gap in space and stepped through, holding the flap open for Kate to enter.

"Argh!" screamed Clarence,

Rafe noted that they'd come out onto into the hallway, right next to Clarence who was dusting cobwebs from the corners of the ceiling.

"Sorry about that, Clarence." Rafe shrugged.

Kate strode into the lounge to find Anthony and Larissa hunched over a ragged and dusty-looking book. At Kate's entrance, Rafe spied Anthony's face scowl, while Larissa subtly closed the book.

"We're going to have to set some ground rules with you turning up," Anthony rumbled. "What are you both doing here?"

Clarence followed them through and stopped next to Rafe, which he found odd when he'd have expected Clarence to make his way to the side of the other Fates.

"We've been to the Silent Chamber as you requesated."

"And what did you find?" Larissa's voice drifting through the room.

"The place is a bombsite," Rafe said. "Sebastian has well and truly destroyed it, and no doubt got away with part of the Book."

"What makes you so sure?" Anthony bristled at the presumption.

"One of the guardians flinched when we mentioned Sorothir's name. They knew the book was there all along." Rafe felt himself getting a little high pitched as he tried to make his point.

"But how did he know it was in there? Or travel through the portal safely?" Anthony grumbled. Rafe noted he wasn't letting go, he was searching for a weakness in Rafe's angle.

"We don't know how he knew it was there, but he blew up the Silent Chamber, using the Cup of Poseidon." Rafe was pleased that his accusation had the desired effect as all three Fates held their mouths open aghast.

"What do you mean?" Clarence squeaked.

"I haven't figured it all out either." Rafe held his palms out, trying to defend his idea.

"Rafe's right." Kate stepped forward. "The pieces of information we have, and limited I know they are, all point to the Silent Chamber being blown up by Sebastian. Combine that with Sorothir's name causing a stir amongst the gatekeepers, and it points to the fact that Sebastian has the second part of the book.

Bang. Bang.

Everyone's head spun in unison towards the door.

"Who should interrupt us?" Anthony stomped to the door.

A male voice echoed in the corridor, followed by footsteps. Anthony emerged with Sherlock in tow wheezing.

"Are you alright, Sherlock?" Larissa placed a hand on Sherlock who bent double trying to catch his breath.

"Jus' a minute."

Clarence pulled a chair over with a screech, then eased Sherlock into it. Sherlock slouched back and closed his eyes.

Everyone around the room stood silently and focused intently on the heaped figure sat down.

"What did he say he wanted?" Kate quizzed Anthony.

"Something about a battle but I couldn't make it out."

As they waited, the room's tension increased with each moment, when finally, Sherlock began to sit up.

"There's... a... battle."

"Between who?" commanded Anthony, his voice edged with tension.

"Jupiter's lot... they started... attacking everyone."

"Why?" Larissa's hand went to her mouth.

"No one... cany tell... from what...I 'erd." He took a deep breath. "Jupiter is leadin'... da Roman god... in HOG right... now firin' on... everyone. He's gone crazy." Sherlock panted.

Rafe thought about how god couldn't be killed, but then again, the angels and other shadow creatures in the area that helped run HOG could be. And although a god may be invincible, they could still be imprisoned forever, take Prometheus for instance.

There was one word from Sherlock that prodded him constantly though. Roman. It was not a coincidence that they were only besides Jupiter's son not long ago. Before he could voice his thought, Kate beat him to it.

"Caesar. We were with Jupiter's son not long ago," Kate exclaimed. "And so was Sebastian."

Emboldened by Kate, Rafe gave his view. "And not long after Sebastian was with Heracles, disguised at Cleon, Zeus disappeared. Somehow Sebastian is using the sons of these god to use the Book of Sorothir."

"It seems though," Sherlock offered, "while Zeus disappeared, Jupiter has lost his mind."

"You're right!" How could he have been blinded by it, Rafe chided himself. "Perhaps the different parts of the book do different things."

"Different parts?" Sherlock frowned.

Rafe chose to ignore the interruption. "The first part of the book he stole from Silevaith enabled him to make Zeus disappear, or perhaps he hasn't disappeared, but Sebastian has control of his body. And the second part, which he has got from the Silent Chamber, has made Jupiter lose his mind."

"So how many parts are there?" Sherlock said again, confused. "And how does he use the offspring of the god to activate the book?"

"There are three parts, but I don't know how he is doing yet."

"But we're a lot closer to solving this than we have ever been," interjected Kate. "So, what do we do now?"

A wall of silence.

"I guess we wait until we find out where he strikes next," soothed Larissa.

"I think we need to look for the last part of book as well," Suggested Kate. "Do you have any ideas where it could be, Rafe?"

He shook his head, as he genuinely didn't know. "Perhaps Megan has a lead."

"Megan?" asked Anthony, ever suspicious.

"Megan Arndell? Well at least that's what I think her surname is."

"The Archess' daughter?" Anthony said incredulously.

"Yes."

"I didn't realise you both knew each other."

"We're working together to try and find the missing pieces. Well single piece now," Rafe corrected himself. "Maybe she has something that can help us."

"In the meantime, I'll gather the other Grey Guardians together," Kate offered. "We'll search for Sebastian. If we find him, we find the two parts of the book he already has."

"And we'll monitor the timeline and let you know if Sebastian enters there again. We have one last chance of stopping him, so when we come calling, be ready, okay?" Anthony nodded towards Sherlock. "You'll need to be ready too."

"I'm always ready." Sherlock puffed up his chest.

Chapter Eighteen

After a brief nap on his bed, it was morning time. He'd forgot he had school that day. He put on his clothes, and went to the kitchen to grab a bite to eat before he had to leave. His dad read a newspaper with a coffee in hand as usual, which he peered over the top of.

"I was getting worried you wouldn't come down, is everything okay?" His dad folded the newspaper down and placed it by his side.

Before he could answer, Kira came in and brushed her shoulder against his back.

"Ah, both of you are here now, great. Grab a slice of toast, we're off in two minutes. And don't forget I need you to be quick getting out of school tonight." Rafe's dad pointed at both Rafe and Kira, emphasising he was serious.

"What for?" Rafe queried.

"I have a parents evening tonight, so I need to get you both home with tea before I go to it."

"I was planning on going to the hospital after school," Rafe said a little sheepishly. "To see Evie, you know."

His dad gave that reassuring smile that said everything would be okay. "Of course. Your mother told me she had woken up, I'm really pleased for you, son, its wonderful news."

"You're quite the ladies' man now, aren't you?" Kira winked.

Rafe felt his face turn red.

"Evie. Kate. Who else?" Kira counted the names on her fingers.

"It's not like that," Rafe spluttered.

"Oh. I'm sure." Kira grabbed her bag and made her way to the hall as their dad stood watching with a slight smirk across his face.

With coffee still in hand, he placed his spare hand on Rafe's shoulder. "Well, I'm happy for you, how do you feel now she is awake?"

"Honestly, Dad? Relieved and tired." Rafe's shoulders sagged a little, the weight of everything starting to take its toll on him.

His dad chuckled. "I know about tiredness, I've had two new-borns remember. Well, when she's feeling better, why not invite her around for tea sometime, hey?" His dad took a slurp of his coffee.

That was actually a nice idea. "Thanks Dad."

The way to school had been the same. His dad listening to some radio station playing music from his childhood. The songs weren't particularly bad, but for some reason, the radio station played the same songs over and over, or at least one's that all sounded the same.

The day at school passed as usual; slow and ponderous. The second hand making its way in circles on the clock. The hour hand moving too slowly. When school finished, and it was time to leave, Rafe sprinted out of the main door and to the main gate. As soon as he rounded the corner, he noticed a figure standing in his way, and he stumbled to a stop, dirtying his shoes in a wet muddy patch of the pavement.

As Rafe wiped the side of his shoes on the wall next to him to get the worst of the mud off, he cast a look at who the object of his angry thoughts were.

Rafe stopped what he was doing and managed to fumble out some words. "What are you doing here?"

"I came to see how things were on your end?" the familiar figure said.

Rafe eyed the wings on her back, which were small and delicate in stature but would nevertheless still attract too much attention amongst the kids coming up behind them.

Megan noticed what he was looking at. "Don't worry about the wings. We have a glamour on us, so they only see me as if I were human."

"That's pretty cool, and a relief."

The wall of kids eager to get out of school swallowed Rafe and Megan up. One of the faces that went past was Kira who cast a puzzled expression and quickly held up three fingers. Rafe managed to spy her smirk before the flow of children pushed her along.

Great, Rafe thought.

"Let's get out of here." Rafe grabbed Megan by the arm to steer her towards the hospital.

"Okay, but where to?"

"Evie's back, so to the hospital."

"That's great news, how did they manage to cure her?" Megan asked as she followed Rafe through kids who were now milling around for their rides home.

How much could he let on?

In the end, Rafe recounted the whole story to her, and to her credit, she only asked a few questions.

“I'm speechless! It's actually quite interesting that the blood held the power to heal. So now Evie will be immortal?” Megan suggested.

“What?” Rafe hadn't really thought about that before.

“Well, she drank the blood, didn't she? And presumably enough not only to heal her but indefinitely.”

“I never really thought about that.”

“Well, I don't know for sure, it's very possible though.”

“I didn't just come to see how you are. I also want to invite you to a meeting that Order Arndell is going to have." Megan stared straight ahead, unflinching in her question.

"Where to?" Rafe frowned at the strange question.

"To see a group of Werefolk, a very powerful one as well."

“Werefolk?” Rafe said incredulously.

“Yes, we will need allies now that a war is starting. My mother has set up a meeting with their leader.” Megan ran her hands through her hair.

“Has she asked for me to be there?” Rafe felt a little nervous being part of something he wasn't invited to. He'd already been on the sharp end of the disdain felt for him from Silevaith and Grainne.

Rafe watched her face closely as she answered. “Not exactly.”

Rafe's heart sunk, and he couldn't help but let escape a groan. “Your mum will crucify me when she sees me.”

“You'll be one amongst many there, and as daughter of the Archess, I can pick who I want to accompany me. Besides, I think it would be good for you to come with me?”

“Really? Why?” Rafe asked.

“You will get to learn more about our world and, in return, you offer something that my angel friends cannot, the ability to move through space and time."

Rafe searched Megan's face for any sign of mocking. To his surprise, she was completely impassive. Rafe realised she was being totally serious in her need for his help.

"Are we expecting trouble then?" Rafe said.

"I don't know, it's not a straightforward meeting. For instance, we've been asked to meet in a large chamber close by a mountain range which is unusual for such a meeting. Usually, it's in a small, secluded place in some building amongst the Werefolk, but the different location has set off warning signals to me and I'd rather be prepared."

Rafe nodded his understanding of the situation.

"We're here now." They reached the hospital.

They entered the sliding glass doors as they parted, then took the lift to the necessary floor, their footsteps echoing along the hall.

Swinging into Evie's room, he instantly checked his step as Evie's parents came into view next to her bed. Her dad had her arm around her mum, which Rafe couldn't help but raise his eyebrows at, having never seen them together before. Perhaps Evie's close brush with death had brought them close together again, Rafe reflected. It's strange how some things can recalibrate what is important in life.

"Oh, hi Rafe," Evie's mum called. "This is Ted, Evie's dad."

"Hi, young man." Ted rounded the bed and shook Rafe's hand a little too eagerly. "I heard you visited often, thank you." Ted then spun towards Megan. "Hi there."

"Hi, I'm Megan," Megan said a little tentatively, taking a step back.

Rafe watched the awkward silence drag out, and then attempted to divert them onto surer footing. "Sorry for intruding, we just came to see Evie." He glanced over at her to see a spoon halfway to her mouth, watching the scene unfold.

It was the first time he had seen Evie so alive, and he'd forgotten how dark her eyes were. Evie placed the spoon back into the bowl and beamed at him. Rafe couldn't hold it back anymore and forgetting anyone else was in the room, he took the last strides to her bed and wrapped his arms around her.

Sitting below his height in bed, she wrapped one arm around his and whispered so only he would hear, "Thank you."

Rafe felt a gentle squeeze.

Rafe heard one of Evie's parents make a gentle cough from somewhere in the room, followed by their excuses to get a drink from the cafeteria.

Releasing Evie, he stumbled with his words, "I... err..."

"*He missed you.* Is what he is trying to say." Megan stood just to the side of him now. He hadn't heard her footsteps.

"Yes... I..." Rafe continued trying to find the right words.

"*He's been so worried about you and he has so much to tell you*. Is what he wants to say now."

Rafe eyed Megan, who smiled fully.

Megan then rolled her eyes. "I'm just trying to speed things up here, I don't have all day."

"It sounds like you have a hell of a story to tell me." Hearing Evie's voice was like a breath of fresh air, filling Rafe with a new lease of life.

"That's an understatement! It's taken me months to figure out how to heal you."

Rafe told Evie about Airmed's blood; it was practically identical to the story he had told Megan on the way to the hospital.

When he finished, he felt the lightest of touches at his elbow. Megan gentle squeezed it. "It's time Rafe, the meeting starts soon."

Rafe sighed, he didn't want to go now.

"You're going, so soon?" Evie said a little sadly.

"Megan has asked me to join her at a meeting between the Arndell Angels and the Werefolk."

"War is coming," Megan added from the side. "Evie, it's been nice to see you again, but it's an important meeting, and we can't be late." Megan gazed at her watch. "Rafe, I didn't realise the time, you need to say goodbye asap."

Rafe felt a nudge in his back.

"Bye." He hugged Evie again, though this time she placed her lips on his cheek and gave him a small peck.

Rafe felt the colour rising up his collar as he stepped back.

"Erm... Bye." Rafe gave an awkward wave which he instantly regretted.

"Come along now." Megan grabbed him by the arm and swung him out of the room. He barely had chance to glance over his shoulder for one last look at Evie, who was sat in bed, her almost black hair framing her small heart-shaped face.

When they were in the corridor, Megan didn't let up.

"Why are we in such a rush?"

"I didn't realise how late we were."

Rafe felt the air escape him as he was yanked into a side room. "What the..." Rafe started but was unable to finish as Megan placed her finger to Rafe's lips.

"Shh," Megan said removing her finger. "Right, you need to transcend us to Castle Arndell."

Rafe just stared at Megan.

"The meeting. And I need you to be quick." Megan checked her watch again.

Rafe opened a slit for them both to step through.

They arrived within the protection of the castle walls, past the boundaries of protection afforded by the enchantments.

The room they entered was Megan's, who brushed past to a side table. She picked up something and pocketed it, he didn't get a look at what it was but she clearly didn't want him to see it.

"Let's go, they will be leaving the courtyard soon," Megan said.

Outside, there was a lot of hustle and bustle with angels moving back and forwards.

"Something is amiss," Megan said as she watched the angels coming and going.

She was right, there was something etched on the faces of the angels that passed them by, barely giving them a glance.

Megan grabbed someone by the arm. The other angel tried to shake Megan off until they locked eyes and the struggle from the other angel dissipated.

"I apologise." The angel bowed his head at the neck. "I did not realise it was you, if I had I would have stopped instantly."

"No need to apologise," Megan said releasing his arm, which the other now rubbed. "What is going on here?" Megan waved her hand around them.

"The Archess has ordered the guard to be doubled and everyone to be on standby. She is now heavily guarded in her chambers with a small entourage," the angel answered.

"Thank you." Megan flicked her head to the side to dismiss the angel. Once he was out of sight, Megan bolted down the aisle leaving Rafe in her wake. Rafe bounded forward, but his legs wouldn't move as quick as Megan's. The tip of her head was bopping down the staircase, to the floor below. Rafe tried to keep up but before he knew it, he'd lost her at a fork in the hall, one path let straight on and another went left.

Panting and hands on his head, he tried to grab his breath as he decided which way was the right way.

Thankfully, he heard something.

"Oi! This way and keep up!" Megan popped her head out from around the corner.

Relieved, Rafe ran as fast as his legs would take him, hobbling down the hall. They went down a long corridor and came to the large wooden doors of the chamber he had been in before. But outside were not two guards but eight from his initial count.

"I said let me in!" Megan yelled.

Rafe joined Megan, clutching his side. There seemed to be a stand-off between Megan and a grisly looking angel with a greying beard. "You may have had orders not to disturb her however you didn't have orders to stop her daughter." Megan stepped around the figure before he could answer and moved towards the Great doors. Rafe was impressed, as all eyes pierced into her back, not one laid a finger on her, so she began to push the doors open with a grunt.

"Well, are you coming or what?" Megan shouted back at Rafe.

Rafe made an awkward leap forward before anyone could challenge him, and stepped in next to Megan. She held the door open for him and slammed it shut once they were both through. The thud of the door echoing around the room drew the attention of its occupants. In the room behind them, it was indeed an entourage of a small number of guests. Walking towards the group, he saw in their midst Grainne, Silevaith, Arabor and Nemor but it was the last figure which all eyes were focused on. A tall angel, slim, straight backed and with dark hair cut close to the scalp. The face was gaunt and the cheeks were caved in, but despite the feral appearance, this angel was at the centre of the group.

The whole group stopped their conversation and gazed towards them, and before anyone could challenge them, Megan strode over to her mum, reached for her hand and caressed it in between hers. Rafe thought it an odd gesture, having never seen affection between Silevaith and her daughter before.

"Mother, what is going on?" Megan asked in a soft voice and casting a nervous look at the stranger in the centre of the group.

Silevaith's eyes darted amongst the others that had gathered, and a smile creased at the edge of her mouth.

Rafe had never seen her smile as such.

"We are blessed, Daughter." Pulling her to the centre of the group. Grainne squinted at Rafe as he stepped in behind.

"This is Sorothir," Silevaith said.

Rafe opened his mouth and let it hang. Sorothir!

Rafe blinked and said the name over and over in his head. Sorothir! Sorothir!

How could this be, Rafe thought and his knees began to buckle. Rafe took a deep breath.

"How?" Megan asked slightly muffled as her hand hid her mouth.

"She has come to help us."

"But... but... how can this be. No one has seen you for thousands of years, everyone thought you were dead?" Megan directed at Sorothir.

Everyone looked towards the tall and dishevelled figure.

"That's because I have been hiding from the world in order to protect you all." The voice was feminine but held no warmth to it. Rafe had always imagined Sorothir to be male with a flamboyant voice, but now thinking about it, he couldn't remember anyone ever calling Sorothir a *him* or *her*.

"I have kept an eye on things from afar, while I hid in the demon realm." Sorothir let the last part hang in the air, apparently this was something she had not shared with the group yet for Rafe heard Grainne suck in a breath between his teeth.

"The demon realm!" Grainne exclaimed. "That place of danger? How did you survive there?"

"By staying out of site and being cunning," Sorothir said plainly.

"Your Order were always the most cunning of us. Well, fair play to you," Arabor commented and inclined his head in respect to her.

This intrigued Rafe, as he had never considered what Order Sorothir might be part of, and she clearly wasn't from Silevaith's or Grainne's. Rafe made a mental note to ask which Order she came from.

A gentle cough came from someone within the group.

"Yes, we must go. Our guests will be waiting for us in the mountains." Silevaith declared.

"But when will we get the third part of the book?" Arabor asked.

"I will take you to it soon. First though, Silevaith has correctly expressed the urgency to build alliances, and it would not do to keep our guests waiting. Especially ones who are renowned for their lack of patience," Sorothir answered coldly.

"As you wish." Arabor took a step back, indicating he had given ground on the point. "I am ready to leave when you are." Arabor's eyebrows pinching together.

The group moved off, and Rafe tried to keep up

At the large doors, Arabor pushed them open with a heave, which moved more easily as the guards on the other side must have realised what had happened and pulled their way also.

The guards parted to the walls. The angel with the beard with grey streaks bowed his head. "Archess."

"Keep the castle on alert," Silevaith ordered before nodding towards Arabor. "My son, you must take command of the castle in my absence."

"I want to come with you." Arabor said pleading.

"I know. But I need someone I can rely on, to keep our Order safe."

Arabor cast a look towards Megan. It was a strange look, and Rafe wasn't sure how to take it.

"Of course, Mother. It will be my pleasure." Arabor puffed out his chest and waved the bearded angel. "Come, Stryger." To which Arabor and the grey streaked guard departed.

"Let's get going," Sorothir said eyeing Arabor's back fade down the hall. "We've wasted enough time."

Walking the hallways, Rafe followed Sorothir's tall slender frame. Although she walked straight as a pole, Rafe bet she was ready to pounce at a moment's notice.

Reaching the courtyard of the castle, they gathered in a loose circle.

"My men will form the vanguard to the Dragus mountains," growled Grainne to everyone.

Dragus mountains, Rafe had never heard of them before.

Grainne had a contingent of ten warriors with him and they rose first.

Next to Rafe stood a young-looking angel. "Hi, what's your name?" Rafe asked her.

She was younger than most angels. Her hair was long under her helmet and her face pointy, reminding him almost of an elf or pixie.

"My name is Elril." She arched an eyebrow, probably curious as to what a mortal was doing amongst them.

"I'm Rafe. It's nice to meet you."

"Likewise," the angel said politely.

Rafe noted the sword at her hip, and by the way she stood, he was sure she was quick with it.

"Can I ask you a question about Sorothir?" Rafe ventured, and seeing no objection he carried on. "What Order was Sorothir part of?"

The next row in front had lifted off to follow Grainne.

"I heard she was part of the Nis," Elril answered.

"Nis?"

"Yes, the Nisassah, they are a small but clever Order renowned for their intelligence, I would keep my eye on that one." She nodded to Sorothir who was now in the air with Silevaith in front of them.

At that moment, Megan came over. "Right, let's go."

Without any further command, the rest of the angels rose into the air to form a rear guard. Except for Rafe and Megan.

"What do we do?" Rafe asked

"Well, I'm not carrying you." Megan handed Rafe a piece of paper with numbers on.

"What's this?" Trying to decipher what they meant.

"Co-ordinates." Rafe frowned at the numbers. "Look, you don't need to understand them, just memorise them and open a portal. You'll see."

Rafe was sceptical but cast the numbers to his mind and thrust with his arms, when he peered through the slit, he was surprised to see a plateau on a mountainside. Feeling a push on his back, he grabbed for a hand behind him and walked through the gap, pulling Megan in behind him.

On the plateau, they were alone.

Rafe made his way to a large boulder and sat looking out into the dark sky. The plateau was littered with sharp grey rocks, dotted with a few tufts of grass here and there. Rafe heard Megan moving around behind him. Casting a glance behind, he saw her looking at the mountain and heard her shout something carried by the wind.

"There's... cave... here..."

Soon afterwards, Rafe felt the presence of Megan sit next to him on the boulder and lean into him. "There's a cave entrance over there; it looks empty, so the Werefolk are either not coming, or are late."

"How long until the others get here?" Rafe wrapped his arms around him, it was bitterly cold.

"About twenty minutes."

Damn, thought Rafe, he would freeze by that time.

Megan must have read his thoughts for she suggested they walk the mountain to keep warm.

After several laps by which Rafe had lost count of, he spied moving shadows in the sky moving shadows. The fire within him stoked brighter as he realised his agony of being cold was about to end.

The vanguard of Grainne's troops landed in front and fanned out to make a perimeter. Then it was Sorothir and Silevaith with a small contingent of soldiers that landed next.

Rafe would later remember that to be the moment, when all hell broke loose.

Megan moved sideways to get a better look and something brushed along Rafe's right side, smashing into one of the angels in front. He fell to the ground in a mass of limbs flailing about.

"Control yourself!" Grainne shouted as he stabbed down at the thing that was attacking the angel. "Demons! Ready yourself!"

Cries of shock rang out from everyone, including Rafe.

Everyone took their weapons out of their sheafs, to the sound of hissing, and formed a ring.

Demons, Rafe thought, what on earth were demons? He eyed a mass of twisted flesh on the floor next to the motionless angel. Rafe felt light headed and took in deep breaths to clear his vision. Focus, Rafe recited to himself. Staring into the night sky trying to locate their assailants, Rafe couldn't help but sway on his feet. The rhythm of it was the only thing that stopped him from running or passing out. Then without warning, a thump came from one side as a large red demon landed. It opened its mouth and gave a shrill cry, the sharp teeth visible inside. Then another thud came from somewhere else, then another and on they went. Rafe tried to count them, and once he had reached a number higher than their own, he stopped. He thought there were twelve surrounding their tight group. When he squinted, he could just make out more lined up behind them. Perhaps a score of them against their group of fifteen.

"Rafe," Megan whispered. "Get ready to make a portal."

Rafe flexed his fingers. "Where to?" Rafe hissed back.

"Anywhere that's safe and away from mortals, in case those things get through."

"Go," a familiar voice commanded from the dark, and at once, the demons launched themselves at the party.

Rafe manoeuvred himself to the centre of the ring, unashamed of his fear of the things. Rafe closed his eyes to block out the snarling mangled faces of the demons that bore down on their group.

Placing his hands together, he could feel his hands begin to shake.

Rafe scrunched up his face, *come on, Rafe!*

He took a deep breath, thrust forward, and to his relief, a slit through time opened up.

He cast a look sideways and yelled at Megan. "It's done, let's go."

Megan withdrew her sword which she had rammed into the mouth of a demon and was now swinging towards one that had come from above. "Megan. It's ready!" Rafe shouted again, feeling his voice go hoarse.

The demon Megan hacked at, collapsed with scream.

Rafe heard a crack from above his head. At first, he thought it was thunder, but when he heard it again, he saw Silevaith with a black whip in hand flail at a demon that had sprung up close to Rafe.

Rafe jumped to the side while ensuring he didn't let go of the portal entrance. Where had that demon come from, Rafe thought, he hadn't even heard it approach.

Silevaith cracked her whip at it again, and this time, it wrapped around its leg. With a tug, it fell to the ground, Rafe saw his opportunity and drew his sword from his belt, and thrust it down. As the skin was thick, it only caused a glancing blow, off its shoulder. A shadow appeared in front, and Megan used a knife to finish off the demon.

"Everyone into Rafe's portal!" Megan shouted.

Rafe tore it open wide and held it open but before anyone could get into it, another portal opened up in front, and Sebastian walked through, his sword in a guard position across his body. Elril, who was now sporting a bloody cut across her cheek, was closest to Rafe and stopped mid step, at the sight of Sebastian.

"Who are you?" Elril snarled.

All around, limbs and bodies moved back and forwards as the skirmishes increased between their small party and the oncoming demons.

Grainne and two of his guards bounded past Elril.

Rafe thought they were all going to collide into Sebastian, but at the last moment Sebastian stepped back, and the tear in fabric from which he had appeared through, vanished.

The moment of hesitation caused by Sebastian's appearance had done its job and now the demons were swarming around them. Rafe had to roll out of the way as one swiped at him with elongated claws. Megan hacked at the arm, causing a howl from the demon.

With no one holding Rafe's portal anymore, the tear in fabric vanished.

Rafe drew his sword and surveyed around them. On the floor lay one of Grainne's guards with a growing pool underneath her, while Grainne and Nemor fought back-to-back, keeping razor sharp claws at bay.

Sorothir, whom Rafe had noticed for the first time since the battle had occurred, leapt into the sky, and with a wave of her arm, a powder scattered across a group of demons that were surrounding her. As the cloud of powder settled on her quarry, they each clawed at their faces and screamed out in a high pitch. They each fell to their knees, clawing at themselves.

What was that powder, Rafe wondered.

He didn't have any more time to contemplate what had happened, as something hard barrelled into him. Rafe hit the ground head first.

Ah, it hurt! Rafe tried to raise himself to his knees, but one of his legs was pinned. Grainne was on top of him trying to hold off a snarling demon, the sharp teeth inching closer to his face. It would only be a matter of seconds before the demons' superior strength enabled its sharp teeth to sink into Grainne.

Not knowing what else to do, Rafe raised his sword in two hands and stabbed around Grainne into the back of the demon. He decided to stab rather than slice for not knowing if a slice would even penetrate the demon's red mottled skin.

To his relief, the short sword was sharp enough to penetrate through the back of the now flailing beast, its back arching. Rafe tried to wrench his sword free but it was firmly wedged in the demon. Clenching his fist until his knuckles went white, he swung as hard as he could, his fist following around in an arc. It crashed into the jaw of the red beast, toppling it sideways, where it lay on the ground shuddering.

Rafe reached out a hand to Grainne who clasped his hand around Rafe's wrist and yanked himself up.

There was no time for talk as another demon sprung at them. Grainne sidestepped and drew a knife from his belt and started stabbing it in the head.

Rafe went around to the now motionless demon and tried to yank his sword free. As he did, he saw his knuckles were a bloody mess with scratches and cuts from where he had punched the demon. He braced his foot on the demon and yanked harder, but it still didn't budge.

A shadow fell over him and a grizzled hand reached out and pulled the sword free. Grainne handed it to him and grumbled something unintelligible.

Feeling safe in Grainne's presence, Rafe took a few moments to survey the battle. Half of the demons were down, but so were some of their own party, and those that were still standing all had injuries.

Sorothir was now flanked by Megan on one side and Silevaith on the other.

Megan spotted Rafe and yelled out, "Rafe make the portal!"

Rafe hobbled over with Grainne, pressed his hands together and tore an opening.

But before anyone could enter, a small line appeared in mid-air and Sebastian jumped through, legs first, he landed a kick on Silevaith who stumbled back. Megan thrust a sword towards Sebastian but before it reached its target, he'd entered another portal and appeared behind Megan.

Sebastian was quick. His speed and skill scared Rafe.

Sebastian's sword arm moved backwards slightly. Rafe thought he was about to strike, so without thinking, Rafe leapt forward to tackle him. Sebastian didn't go down, but his knee was forced to bend as Rafe collided onto Sebastian's leg, making the sword thrust miss and slice through Megan's arm instead.

"Argh!" yelled Megan, reaching for her arm.

Sebastian spun out of Rafe's grip and made another portal. This time, Rafe felt rather than saw him, as he appeared behind Rafe and shoved him to the ground.

"Stay down, Rafe," Sebastian said quietly. "I don't want to hurt you."

Sorothir thrust her hand in her sleeve and spun backwards to lunge at Sebastian. Again, Sebastian vanished into a portal.

Sebastian's ability to open portals at will and at speed, was mind blowing to Rafe. If they made it out of here, he wanted to learn to do that.

Without a pause in the battle, Rafe saw the familiar line open up behind and above Sorothir. Rafe made to shout out a warning but was barged from the side by an angel being attacked by a black demon, its tail whipping back and forwards. Sebastian landed on top of Sorothir, pinning her to the ground, Rafe watched as he stamped on the hand holding the knife. Sebastian grabbed Sorothir from behind and hauled her up without an effort, dragging her backwards, a plume of dust followed as Sorothir flailed in protest.

With Sorothir's capture, the demons backed off. Now that calm befell the battlefield. Rafe could see that the demons had been whittled down significantly, with many on the floor or having fled. Made up of different colours and twisted limbs and sharp spikes, no two were the same, the demons took a step back towards their master. And Rafe took advantage of the lull to heave in deep breaths, he was exhausted.

"It's over now," Sebastian called out with Sorothir firmly clutched in his grip. "Put down your weapons."

No one moved. Rafe could only hear the heavy breathing from those around him.

"Sebastian," Rafe pleaded and took a step forward.

"Rafe." His face softened. "You should not have come here." His face scrunched up. "Why are you doing this?" Rafe asked.

"Since time started, the gods have treated everyone else like second class beings. They treat us as though we are beneath them! Meaningless! We are all pawns to their games while they sit in their halls making wagers with our lives. Lives that we only have one shot at. They kill as they please, they torture as they please, and they make all suffer, both shadow creatures and humans. WE ARE SLAVES TO THEM!" Sebastian shouted uncontrollably, spittle came from his mouth. Rafe had never seen Sebastian like this before. He was usually calm and meticulous. "You should not have come here, Rafe, I don't want you to die."

Then the penny dropped for Rafe, Sebastian didn't really want to kill them all but was being forced to.

"Sorothir here can take me to the final place of where the book is, then we will be free of the gods. They will be mortals like us." Sebastian went on, tightening his arm around Sorothir's neck.

"How do you know so much about the book?" Silevaith called out with her whip still in hand.

Sebastian grinned and cast a glance at Sorothir whose head was down. "Should I tell them or you?" Sorothir did not make a move.

"Sorothir made the book from knowledge she learned in the demon realm," Sebastian said a little smugly. The whole group started to murmur, even Rafe couldn't help himself and took in a sharp breath. "Yes, you heard me, Sorothir learned demon magic, or blood magic if you prefer. That's where I learned her secret, in the Demon Realm from a Demon Prince."

"You met a Demon Prince and survived?" Grainne exclaimed while leaning a little awkwardly to one side.

"I had an interesting proposition from them, and by sharing our knowledge together, it has brought us closer to bringing down our slavers. Removing their foot from our throats." Sebastian had the fury back in again.

"You are playing with fire by allying with the demons," Grainne shot back.

"It doesn't matter what you think anymore, the doorway to the demon world has been opened, and we will bring an army through. If you stand against us, we will go through you as well."

Rafe knew what was coming soon. He cast his mind to Kate and Evie, knowing he would miss them both. Then there was his family, they meant more to him than he'd previously realised.

"And with Sorothir here, we will now be able to get the rest of the book. Oh, don't look so disgusted, you lot, I don't plan to torture it out of her, I don't need to after all. The first two parts in themselves are enough to get me the last part of the book. One part controls the body, the other the mind, together I can force Sorothir to take me to it." Everyone was watching Sorothir, whose eyes were wide, and her bare-headed scalp was beaded with sweat.

Then Sorothir did something strange, Rafe wasn't sure if he had seen it right. He squinted to see if she did it again but instead, he saw her lips part.

"What did she say?" Rafe whispered to Megan.

"What?" Megan said irritably.

But before he could answer, Sorothir grabbed for her boot, which were large and black encompassing her shin and calf. From within, she withdrew something, then thrust it towards her mouth.

"Now!" someone roared.

"Rafe do it!" yelled Megan.

Rafe twisted around and thrust his hands behind him, opening a gateway. "In everyone!" Rafe yelled.

Silevaith shouted, echoing Rafe's order, "go, quickly into the portal." Before flailing her whip around in arc to hold the advancing demons who had begun to move forwards again.

One by one, they all piled in through the portal until only Silevaith and Rafe were left.

"Come on Archess," Rafe called.

But Silevaith either didn't hear or ignored him. She was staring at Sorothir, who was now motionless at the feet of Sebastian. Rafe noticed how he too looked equally baffled at what had happened to Sorothir.

However they had little time left.

What Rafe did next, he knew would cause scorn later, but he remembered a quote from somewhere that said *indecision was worse than making the wrong decision*. So, without warning Silevaith, Rafe grabbed her by the shoulder and pulling her after him, as he fell through the portal.

Rafe landed at first with a crunch on the gravelled floor underneath and then he felt the air being hit out of him, as Silevaith landed on him in a pile of black.

Rafe's hands couldn't help but brush against the stretched-out wings of Silevaith. They felt light but also brittle as though made of lightweight steel.

Silevaith rolled away from him, and pushed herself onto her two feet, holding his gaze with a scowl.

Rafe tried to splutter out an apology that sounded more like a squeak.

"Mother!" Megan ran over and hugged her and the scowl melted away.

Chapter Nineteen

Rafe sat on the bench watching Evie, as she crouched low to the ground.

She'd spied a dragonfly, stark blue, hovering near a reed in the pond that they sat around. They'd taken a stroll to the park, the one close to their house as he needed to clear his head before he did his school work. It was Sunday night and he hadn't done his work for tomorrow, which was becoming a bit of a habit lately and not going unnoticed by his teachers and parents. He'd been attempting it when he heard a knock on his door, and there on his doorstep was a picture like nothing he had seen before. Rafe hugged her the moment he realised it was Evie, and was relieved when she returned the hug back equally hard.

Evie naturally wanted filling in so they had taken a leisurely walk to the park.

"It's beautiful, isn't it?" Evie whipped her head around with a smile.

"It is," he looked at her, thinking both the dragonfly and Evie were.

When the dragonfly departed, Evie strolled over to the bench, lifted her knees and nuzzled into the arm of Rafe.

"How do you feel?" Rafe asked.

"Quit asking me that, I'm still fine. I'm better than ever, in fact, that god's blood you gave me must be good." Evie chuckled.

"I wonder what powers it gave you?" Rafe queried.

"Well, I for one have no intention of finding out. I am keeping safe from now on."

"Sounds like a plan." Rafe gave a little laugh himself, he'd been feeling giddy the whole way to the park.

"So, we're alone now with no one passing us in the street or interrupting. Tell me what happened." Evie searched Rafe's face, her dark eyes darting back and forwards.

So, Rafe told her everything. He listed it off monotonously as though it was old news, only when he got to recent events, did he feel himself become animated.

"After the battle with Sebastian, Silevaith took us back to her castle. We sat in a private side room patching our wounds. We sat in silence for a long time, no one daring to speak to Silevaith except for Grainne. Apparently Sorothir told Silevaith that the first part of the book which she hid with Silevaith has the power to control the body, the second part that was in the portal of the Silent Chamber, controlled the mind, while the third part controlled the soul, and could kill a god."

"Did Sorothir say where the last part of the book was held?" Evie asked, a little hopefully.

"I asked, and apparently Sorothir didn't want to reveal its location to anyone. Except there was some off comment she made which Silevaith thought was curious, that it was hidden, '*where even time could not touch it.*'" Rafe said the last part with a spooky voice. "Whatever that means."

"That's ominous," Evie said as they both sat in silence. Rafe was trying to solve it but came up with nothing. Perhaps it was somewhere in the timeline, he mused.

"Also, Sebastian told us that the books use blood magic, also known as demon magic."

"Blood magic?" Evie scrunched up her face.

"Apparently, Sorothir learned how to use blood magic while hiding in the demon realm. Which in itself is interesting, how did she even get there, survive, and then learn it, I doubt we'll ever know. The last we saw of Sorothir was motionless at the feet of Sebastian, if she's still alive then Sebastian has her but for all we know, she could be dead."

"So, Sebastian got hold of Zeus' blood and Jupiter's blood, which I presume he then used with the book?"

"Yes." Rafe was about to tell her his theory when she beat him to it.

"Heracles and Caesar!" Evie punched Rafe playfully. "Gosh I am good."

Rafe smiled and had to admit she was, she'd figured it out quicker than he had.

"You know, you are incredible to work that out so quickly. I wonder at what point he got their blood?" Rafe felt Evie snuggle in tighter.

"Well, when you see him next, make sure it's the first thing you ask him," Evie said.

"So, what next then?"

"School tomorrow. Until you're called by The Fates again." Evie sighed.

Epilogue

Sebastian sat in a café sipping a coffee, watching people scramble about outside with their umbrellas as the rain poured down. Even though the torrential downpour had been forecast, the residents of this city had been undeterred, still going out in their droves, wrapped in their waterproofs and prepared with umbrellas. He watched as the weather turned, everyone passing his window huddled into the collars of their jackets, some had their umbrellas out already. Sebastian allowed time to pass by playing game; of evaluating everyone's personality based on the umbrella and the coats they wore. Whether they were bright, dull or patterned, they each portrayed who the owner was, providing an insight into their lives.

Sebastian reached for his drink and took a sip, but coming up empty after a small mouthful. Peering in, he saw he'd finished it. Shame, he thought, it was a nice drink. He must have been here a while without realising it. He'd come in to think about the events from the other day, when he'd been forced to confront Rafe and the angels from Orders Arndell and Galad.

A shadow called from above. "Sorry but we're about to shut now," said a waitress in a black top, who had a simple face, with bushy curls sprouting up over her ears. "Was everything okay?"

Sebastian saw behind her, that the tables were wet from being wiped and the chairs were stacked. He hadn't noticed her clearing up. Peering at his watch, he was surprised to see it so late. Even if he didn't want to go back to where he was staying, he had no choice, he couldn't make any more excuses to avoid the inevitable.

Sebastian sighed and heaved himself up. "It was lovely thanks, I really enjoyed it, thank you."

The waitress stepped back to allow him through. "You're welcome, hopefully we'll see you again here."

When Sebastian reached the door, he glanced back to see her beaming at him. Even though he would love to have another cup from here again sometime, he knew it was unlikely to ever happen. The plans he had set in motion were coming to an end soon and it had become abundantly clear, that there was only one way this was going to end.

As he crossed the threshold of the café to the pavement, the rain drenched him, and Sebastian grimaced as he nestled into the collar of his coat.

He walked the streets towards where he was staying, an apartment in a high-rise building down the road, which he had booked online for a short term let using false details.

Rounding a corner to the twinkling lights of his apartment block, he noticed a bus stop with a handful of people huddled under the protection of its small plastic roof. And there *he* was, just standing a few strides from the huddled group as a hooded shadow. He could tell it was him from the tall height and the way he just stood still in the rain, not moving, while everyone around him moved like a tide. Sebastian checked his steps and tried to make out the face in the darkness of the sky, hoping he was wrong.

Sebastian crossed the road, watching out for cars which passed with their lights. When he reached the other side of the pavement, his foot stepped in a puddle. Sebastian cursed and shook his foot. He was about to set off again when he noticed the figure standing in front of him now, blocking his path.

The same figure had been next to the bus stop, a good foot taller than him, and a good foot wider and covered in a hooded cloak, which would have seemed out of place in the daylight and clear skies of a normal day.

Sebastian heard a screech from behind, he dared not turn to see what it was, but when the noise stopped behind him, and he was bathed in light, he realised the bus had arrived.

With the added light, a glint of something shining came from under the hood of the figure in front. And then he knew for certain, it was *him*.

Sebastian moved away from the hooded figure and walked casually to a canopy located on an adjacent building. He didn't look back, knowing the figure would be following him. When he reached the sanctuary of the canopy, Sebastian leaned against the wall and slid his hand to the dagger hidden at his waist.

The figure, clad in black, stood a few feet away and didn't remove its hood, it never did but it spoke in the same threatening voice. "We want to know when you'll find the third part of the book?" It said in a sinister voice.

"Not long now," Sebastian lied.

"Our patience is running low." The figure let the last word draw out.

"I found two parts of the book, didn't I?" Sebastian knew he sounded pathetic when he said it but he needed to give himself some breathing space.

"When I first came to you and told you of the secret my master, The Demon Prince, knew, you agreed to use this knowledge to our mutual benefit. You knew of the consequences of failure, so in case you've forgotten, I'm here to remind you." It didn't say anything further but walked into the night and blended in with the crowds moving back and forwards.

"What have I done? It's gone too far."

Sebastian closed his eyes and raised his chin to allow the water to fall down onto his face, and wash away the tension and fear. He balled his fists, and, without looking, he threw one arm to the side to punch the wall, knowing he would graze his hand and open up bleeding wounds.

Newsletter and About Author

For new, giveaways and latest releases please subscribe to my newsletter via:

www.facebook.com/JoshuaMortimerAuth

If you have enjoyed reading my books please consider leaving a review of this book with your ebook retailer.

About The Author

Joshua Mortimer was born in the Isle of Man and has 5 brothers. He moved to the United Kingdom at the age of 18 when he studied Politics at Lancaster University. Inspired by his mum, Carole Mortimer, who is a prolific romance author, he began writing in 2013 while living in London. What started off as a few pages in the evenings after work and during lunch breaks would become an 8 year project to write The Grey Guardian and the start of The Book Of Sorothir Series. Married to Esther, they have 3 beautiful children that inspire them every day.

Titles in Book of Sorothir Series

The Grey Guardian

The Angel Guardian

Printed in Great Britain
by Amazon

61818302R00139